AESTHETIC MOTIVE

THE MACMILLAN COMPANY
NEW YORK · BOSTON · CHICAGO
DALLAS · ATLANTA · SAN FRANCISCO

MACMILLAN AND CO., LIMITED
LONDON · BOMBAY · CALCUTTA
MADRAS · MELBOURNE

**THE MACMILLAN COMPANY
OF CANADA, LIMITED**
TORONTO

AESTHETIC MOTIVE

BY

ELISABETH SCHNEIDER

→≫ • ≪←

NEW YORK

The Macmillan Company

1939

PRINTED IN THE UNITED STATES OF AMERICA
AMERICAN BOOK—STRATFORD PRESS, INC., NEW YORK

PREFACE

IN THIS essay I have undertaken to present a theory of aesthetic experience which differs considerably from the theories now current. It is not a complete aesthetic system or an organized philosophy of art, even in outline. I doubt, indeed, whether a satisfactory philosophy of art can be evolved until we have answered with a little more certainty than we have yet done the question of why man creates and enjoys art. This book is concerned, then, solely with a theory of aesthetic motive, and it takes up the other more familiar questions of aesthetics and criticism only as they are seen to be affected by that motive.

For the development of the ideas presented here, I owe a debt incalculably great to my friends Miss Abbie Huston Evans, Mrs. Elizabeth McCord de Schweinitz, Mr. Karl de Schweinitz, and Dr. Barrows Dunham. Without their contribution in thought and discussion, this book would have contained many more oddities and rather less soundness than it now shows. I am much indebted also to Dr. Stuart Robertson and Dr. John Kern for some valuable suggestions, and for their kindness and care in reading the proof; and to Dr. Hughbert Hamilton for furnishing me with a useful illustration from biology. I wish to acknowledge here another debt, although it is a very old one, to Mr. Roger Sessions, who many years ago drew my interest to the theoretical aspects of art through an analytical study of music.

E. W. S.

February, 1939

CONTENTS

CHAPTER ONE

AESTHETIC THEORY AT PRESENT

In a century that has increased our knowledge—if not our wisdom—almost incalculably in certain directions, it is remarkable how stationary our views have been in others. This is a platitude, and perhaps none but the naïve is surprised if the world stands still. Yet many persons interested in literature or art must have wondered that no acceptable theory has even now been evolved to explain the function of art in man's life. This is not to say that none has been offered; only that none has received universal, or even general recognition. The four most potent revolutionizers of modern thought—the biological theory of evolution, the theory of relativity and its allied developments in physics, the Marxian theory of history and the state, and the Freudian theory of the unconscious—all these together might have been expected to shock or jostle aesthetic theory into a new position. They have done so in part, but separately and, each in terms of the other, irreconcilably.

Most anthropologists and many Marxists, for example, believe that art is and should be a tool of society; that its function is to create or tighten solidarity within a social group or to maintain or bring about a particular form of society; that, in fact, if art is living and vital it always tends and should tend to some outcome in social action and that if it does not do so it is sterile; that for the sake of civilization the artistic value of any work of art must be partly if not wholly judged by the rightness of the social action toward which it tends. The Freudians, on the other hand, building partly upon Schiller's "play" theory, see art as the adult's version of childish pretense-playing, a form of wish-fulfillment related to dreams and to fantasy or daydreams.[1] The mere statement of these two ideas side by side must suggest to us at least the possibility that neither theory has quite reached down to the basis of artistic creation. And one wonders if there is not some point of view other than the professed Marxist's or psychoanalyst's from which the conflict between these and perhaps other theories of art would appear less sharp or would even disappear altogether.

Quite as much as the history of philosophy itself, the history of aesthetics has seen a series of confused and contradictory ideas, many of them throwing important light on the artistic process, but many of them also tending to cancel each other out by contradictory premises. A final solution of all these problems, of course, awaits the final solution of all philosophical and all scientific problems, and this most of us have to content ourselves with putting off to the infinitely distant and probably unattainable future. But that does not imply the impossibility of some better synthesis of our knowledge than we have achieved in the past.

Wherever we find often recurring contradictory views upon a subject, we have in the end to ask ourselves two questions or attempt to solve our problem by one of two

---

[1] I summarize the theories at this point briefly and therefore somewhat loosely.

means: either we must find a point of view from which the apparent contradiction can be seen to vanish, or we must conclude that one at least of the contradictory ideas is false; and we can be satisfied of this latter conclusion only if we can not only show it somewhat probably to be false, but can also find a good explanation for the persistence of the false idea in the minds of men. It is quite possible, of course, that our knowledge does not at present permit us to reach satisfactory conclusions about any of the major problems of art, that no common ground is at present available. But the search for it is at least worth making. In the realm of aesthetic theory many of the contradictory ideas have been truisms often repeated, not apparently reconcilable with each other, and yet believed —not merely by opposing schools of thought, each of which has held to its own theory—but believed at the same time by the same people, and sometimes pretty universally. New attempts at an aesthetic theory might well be tested at least in part by the light which they throw or fail to throw upon this mass of contradiction and conflict.

There is, in the first place, the old question of art and morality, a question which, though as ancient perhaps as art itself, is by no means dead; which seems, in fact, to grow more complex all the time. Over and over again we find the idea of beauty associated with truth and goodness. This was common in Greek thought; and in Christian Europe for many centuries the prevailing idea was that good art must be edifying. By the modern world this view has been challenged; yet it is more prominent today among critics of literature and art than it was twenty years ago. For, as we have just said, one of the prevailing theories among anthropologists and sociologists today is that the primary function of art is a social one: that it serves partly as a repository for the culture of a society, but even more as a means by which society may control the individual, may enforce or make acceptable to him its collective will, for the collective good. This is merely a non-moralistic restatement of the moralist theory of art.

But in spite of the strong tradition for moral usefulness, an opposite tradition has come to be equally strong in other quarters. Its most extreme form—the "art for art's sake" theory that a work of art, having nothing to do with life, possesses an absolute, not a teleological value—stands somewhat discredited at present. But the majority, perhaps, of the best critics of the past century and a half have been insisting that art is always "disinterested", which comes to almost the same thing; have been busy showing us that Milton was at his best as a poet when he was not trying to justify his theology and that Spenser was a great poet not because of, but possibly even in spite of, his moral allegory. They have insisted too that great music is "beautiful" in a way that has nothing to do with good or evil or even with "truth" in any unmystical sense of that word.

We have here only the barest mention of the commonplaces that have been uttered and argued on this subject. Confusion is increased by the fact that, though the theories stand opposed, the contenders rarely remain altogether faithful to their own side.

Another vast problem is that of form in art: What constitutes form? what is its function? and how important is it? Its importance is generally thought to be immense; yet we are often shown the contrast between ancient classical art which depends on "balance, symmetry, form", and the romantic art which dwells not on form but on the "expressive", the "characteristic", or "self-expression". Both are thought to be art, but we are left wondering what they have in common to make them so. Again, what is the significance of the recurrent ateleological definitions of form? The principle of unity in variety led Plato to the equilateral triangle as the most beautiful of forms. The eighteenth century was again looking for the most perfectly beautiful form and found it sometimes in the circle, sometimes in a gentle double curve resembling the cyma. And today Mr. Birkhoff finds that beauty conforms to a mathematical formula. The measure of aesthetic value, he has discovered, is expressed by the formula $M = \dfrac{O}{C}$. By means of this ratio the value of any given work of art may be accurately measured.

There are a few other notorious aesthetic puzzles that may be mentioned. Why are the arts not progressive—or are they? In science, the progress has been interrupted only by a partial or complete overthrow of a civilization. Why has not art in the same manner improved steadily? Why have Greek sculpture and architecture been unsurpassed in beauty by the moderns? Why has not modern painting improved upon that of the Renaissance? Why have we not written better drama or poetry than Shakespeare's? And has music been a succession of improvements from Palestrina through Bach, Beethoven, Brahms, to Stravinsky?

If the solution of this problem is, as many writers believe, that each artist restates eternal truths in terms of his own generation—then what are these eternal truths? and why does each generation find at least as much "inspiration" in the art of the past as in that of its own time? Moreover, although there is no general agreement that contemporary work in any art is superior to all past art, nevertheless there are generally recognized and unmistakable changes from age to age in what gives aesthetic pleasure, as in the history, for example, of musical concords, where we find that the now pleasant concord of a major third was once a discord. There are, to be sure, those who believe that the pleasure derived from old writers and artists is merely a conventional cult, without reality, and that actually art of the present is always superior to that of the past. But in general those most intensely interested in art do not feel this to be true.

Again, in another direction, if art is escape from reality, or wish-fulfillment, why (this is another very old question, answered many times) does the tragic or the ugly give pleasure, and why does very little of the greatest art represent human happiness? Or are those critics right who say that the artist represents not the unreal but the profoundest of truths—and are most of these truths unpleasant? And if this is so, why do we constantly speak of "creating the illusion" in art?

These questions could be extended almost indefinitely, but perhaps there have been too many of them already. They have been introduced, however, because it seems unfortunately true that in modern books and theories about aesthetics the attempt is most often, not to discover what is at the bottom of all that has been written and thought and felt on the subject by philosophers or artists or their public, but instead to find a place for art that shall conform to the author's own special set of interests. If he is a psychologist he tries only to fit art into behaviorism or psychoanalysis or whatever his particular school may be. Or his theory is sociological, or historical. The consequence is that along with much greater light on the subject we have much greater confusion too than the study of aesthetics has seen in the past.

The same confusion and contradiction are found in the writing of the more technical philosophers and aesthetic theorists. We should require a great deal more technical discussion and more space than I wish to use here for the purpose, to point them out; but the same explosion of contradictions would occur, and the same unanswerable questions would arise if we should set up Croce, Santayana, and—say—Clive Bell, to be reconciled with one another.

There is a hope that experimental psychology may some day throw light upon all the confusion. This is only a hope for the future, however, and very little help in the present. It is true that since Fechner published his work in 1876, many experimental psychologists have prowled about in this territory. They have done more: they have performed careful experiments and have tabulated results that are often of considerable interest. But none of the results thus far obtained is of any theoretical value for aesthetics. The trouble has generally been that the experiments are conducted without a sufficiently definite aim, and upon no clearly conceived hypotheses. And the consequence is that they often prove nothing, or nothing that the experimenter thinks they prove; or else that they test a response which is very likely not an aesthetic response but something different.

A number of experiments, for instance, have been conducted with the purpose of studying people's color preferences, either in simple colors or in two-color combinations. The subjects of the experiments are asked to designate as pleasant or unpleasant, or to arrange in an order of preference, colors exhibited generally as varied pieces of paper against a gray, black, or white background. Their choice in simple colors may then be compared with their judgment of the same color when combined with another. The conclusions of such experiments need not be taken up here. They are generally not very clear-cut. And before they could be said to have significance for the study of aesthetics, several implied assumptions would need to be established: for instance, that the "affective" response to one [1] or two solid colors presented in this way is in fact an aesthetic response and is therefore the same in kind, if not in degree, as the response to a painting by Titian; or that all persons are equally or almost equally suitable subjects in whom to study aesthetic experience.[2]

Other problems such as rhythm in poetry or prose have been studied. The most elaborate machinery has been worked out for recording duration of time in the utterance of separate syllables of speech, with every sort of aid to ensure that the reader shall feel perfectly natural as he reads. He practices, and many precautions are taken to make the recording scientifically perfect. But another assumption is tacitly made by reason of the choice of a reader: the man who with all this care reads lines from Shakespeare into the machine is a psychologist or, in another case, three or four psychologists, an elocution in-

[1] Actually, of course, the experiment does not test one's preference for a single color, since the background, however neutral, cannot be ignored by the mind, and the observer is therefore always seeing a combination of colors.

[2] I have sketched these experiments so briefly as to do them some injustice. In many instances the experimenters are thoroughly aware of the problems involved. Often they take care to draw no specific aesthetic conclusions but only conclusions about the "affective value" of the colors to the given individuals. But even at best, as scientific experiment, they are full of holes.

structor, and an English instructor. Yet the results are given either specifically or by implication as *Shakespeare's* rhythms—measured in hundredths of a second. And the experimenters would doubtless brand as fussy or unrealistic any critic who contended that the art of oral reading is almost never mastered to the perfection of a hundredth of a second, even by elocution or English instructors.

These are typical instances. The science of the experimental psychologist, as applied to aesthetics, is still in its infancy; and perhaps it will not grow out of that until more generalizing minds have provided it with a few at least tentatively acceptable hypotheses to work upon. At any rate, it has nothing in the way of results as yet to contribute to our understanding of art.

That means that those of us who think we have any general ideas on the subject should perhaps air them, if only as bait for greater fish. If enough speculation is produced, some fragments of it here and there may be found to correspond, and thus perhaps in time we shall work out a more consistent theory than we now have. At worst, in the present state of thought in aesthetics, one or two more theories lying about will hardly make the confusion any more profound.

The point of view which I shall present did not arise, it should be freely admitted, from a contemplation of all the problems of aesthetics and a direct attempt to find a harmonizing and unifying theory. It arose, as most such things do, from a variety of reading and experience, but became crystallized, apparently quite by accident, in consequence of a dinner-table conversation about a poor and now quite forgotten play which happened to raise for me quite sharply, some ten years ago, the old questions of simplification and form, and of what it is that we do to living events, and why, when we impose artistic form upon them. It also raised the question of where form ends and content begins; and of whether the two are as antithetical, or even as distinct and different, as we are accustomed to suppose. For it brought to mind the paradoxical truth that, in this play as in other and better works of art, that which the author did *not* put into the work as *content* constituted, by the very fact of its omission, a great part of the *form*.

CHAPTER TWO

THE AESTHETIC AS SYMBOL

I will sing one one-e-ry.
What is your one-e-ry?
One and one is all alone, and evermore shall be so.
(English Folksong, quoted from K.
Gilbert's *Studies in Recent Aesthetic)*

THE temper of modern philosophy, both among the learned and in the world at large, places certain difficulties in the way of the artist and the student of art. The greatest of these perhaps is a tacit assumption that man either is or ought to be primarily rational; that he lives by the light of reason or that he can gradually be taught to live by it. This almost worshipful belief in intelligence places on the defensive anyone who talks of "emotion". Even psychologists, whose theories are generally founded upon a belief in the power of feeling to determine human action, are most often apologists, in both senses of that word, for emotion.

Art, on the other hand, is almost universally regarded as having its foundation in man's emotional nature. And so, in spite of much lip service paid to it at the present time, the artist is placed on the defensive and is expected to prove his value. He is asked to harness our emotions in the service of our intellect, or to animate us in our efforts to establish a more rational life for man. Or he is supposed to provide a safety valve for the as yet unhar-

11

nessed emotions, diverting them into harmless channels. But the artist himself rarely feels that this is an adequate account of his function. He does not feel that his is an inferior faculty working in the interests of a higher one. And I think that there is a biological and psychological point of view which upholds him, though it may, at the same time, turn one or two other of our common assumptions upside down.

The aesthetic impulse appears to be exclusively the possession of man. There may possibly be some rudimentary traces of it among animals; but, if so, they are so slight that no one has been able to establish their presence with certainty. For this reason I think it is profitable to turn to what we know of biology, evolution, and primitive psychology for the purpose of seeing what there may be in the transition from animal to man that might account for the development of aesthetic experience. We can return from such an inquiry with an hypothesis only, and not a proof. But since this hypothesis has furnished the background (not, however, the foundation) of much of the theory that I shall present later, I should like to retrace it here.

In doing so I shall drop, for the moment, the assumption naturally dear to our hearts that man is the peak, the summit and climax of the evolutionary process, that evolution has been at work developing ever higher forms, the criterion of that "higher" being the quality which we call intelligence. This is not to deny that man is superior to the rest of creation. Only, the difficulty of defining the word *superior* in terms acceptable, for example, both to the Christian and to the scientific mechanist is too great to be worth attempting if the assumption is not required. We may mean by it superiority in some ateleological sense; or we may mean, as the biologist does, better adaptation than other forms of life, for survival. The fact of man's superiority in this latter sense we all take for granted except on occasions when some unwelcome pessimist, generally an entomologist, threatens us with extinction at the hands or mandibles of that other highly developed branch of the evolutionary tree, the insect world, with its elaborately specialized "instinct".

The prime difference between our own development and that of other forms of animal life that may be typified by the insects lies in our different ways of handling experience. In the insect, experience is stored and transmitted genetically:[1] in man it is stored and transmitted largely through social institutions and is therefore acquired by the individual after birth. This contrast is only relative, of course: both insect and man in some degree use intelligence as well as instinct. The advantage, for survival, of man's method is held to be its flexibility, the fact that intelligence enables him to alter his behavior to fit altered circumstance or environment, and to "choose" his way of dealing with a situation after that situation has presented itself. He does not, like the squirrel, continue to bury nuts out of a nut-burying instinct even though he inhabits a tropical region where no winter comes. Now an insect, in carrying on its very specialized activities, is probably not conscious of a goal in what it does. The young bee probably does not "know" that winter is coming—or even what winter is—when she stores her honey. She is urged by impulses from behind, not by visions ahead. Yet, when winter comes, it feels

[1] It is immaterial to our discussion whether this is true actually and as if *purposively* or only in *effect*, as will be the case if the theory of chance and natural selection continues to be accepted. All that is required is that it should be true in *effect*.

natural to her and right, even perhaps familiar—at any rate, not strange. So we may guess.

The race for survival is not yet won. At present there are more insects than men, or indeed than mammals; and insects have adapted themselves to living, probably, under more varieties of physical condition than have mammals. It is at least conceivable that the greater advantage for survival lies in instinctual adaptation. It is conceivable, further, that man's most valued intelligence is but a substitutional development, forced into prominence and activity in consequence of a genetic loss.

In other words, it is quite possible that the general trend of evolution may have been in the direction of an increasing power to transmit more and more special experience through genetic means. In general, those mutations which should add to this power would have greater survival value than those which did not. But, we may suppose, among the many mutations, one occurs in an otherwise advanced and fit form, in which some of that instinctive "knowledge", not all, is missing, and in which the power to transmit it genetically is reduced. The creature still has the will to survive (whatever that may be), and under favorable circumstances may survive. His decisions are not all made for him in his blood.[1] He lives and acts, but more variably than his ancestors. They too had some small power of learning within their individual life span, and of making "decisions" in the face of circumstance. He uses what of this he has; he survives—not so easily as his relations probably—but he does (or one of him does) survive and reproduce. By contrast with his

[1] I am using terms that would apply only to mammals, but this is merely for convenience and simplification. Such changes would rather have occurred in very early stages of evolution.

brothers, then, he finds that his intelligence—his power, that is, of learning to respond differently to varying conditions—is now of more value to him because of what he has lost. And in his descendants—to take a huge and sudden leap in time, telescoping some millions of generations—this quality tends to increase as it had not done in other biological forms—by natural selection, we may suppose—because of its present substitutional use.

We have traveled a long way from aesthetics, and have been riding a possibly quite dubious conjecture. But there is room for many conjectures at present in the area between psychology and biology. And although this particular one need not be accepted and is not essential to our main purpose, it does bring forcibly to mind one truth that I think is important to realize and accept fully: that man in the course of evolution has experienced considerable loss as well as gain, and that this loss must almost certainly have had an influence of some kind upon his psychic make-up. The perhaps roughly concomitant growth of intelligence and loss of instinct, which means the substitution of action determined more and more by the organism's awareness of a changing outside world for the undeviating and so unhesitating type of action which is predetermined within the organism—this change could not occur alone. Perhaps its greatest consequence would be in developing the illusion, if not the actuality, of free will and responsibility, and, along with these, self-consciousness. This means that the *individual* tends to develop. But so, eventually, does the group—the family and society: there must be some way of transmitting experience or the species does not survive, and with man this way has become more largely social and less exclusively instinctual.

Now if intelligence had completely superseded instinct, and had done so with such entire success that every former function of instinct were now more satisfactorily performed by intelligence, this might have been the only important psychological result—and a profound and revolutionary enough one it is, surely. But that was not the case. Very likely, *in general*, the wisdom acquired through our intelligence and our social institutions is much more useful to us than inherited patterns of behavior would be, but this still does not at every point successfully take the place of instinct. With all man's intelligence, for example, his chance of life as well as his convenience would often have been better served if he had had the home-finding or geographical instinct of a bird. We may easily imagine what an early start navigation would have made if we had had no more than a bird's fear of getting lost.

We still have, it is true, the primary instincts, such as hunger—those essential for survival. But they are mainly instincts of need; and the more specialized instincts, which teach how to satisfy those needs, we have largely lost. A consequence of this mingled loss and gain would inevitably be, I think, that another universal element of experience (universal in animal and man) must have increased immeasurably, the element called by psychologists "ambivalence", a mingling or alternation of attraction and repulsion toward any experience. Man has a strong sense of superiority to the rest of creation. But he has also a sense of insecurity, an inevitable accompaniment of his power of "choice" or "free will". Life no longer seems fixed in its groove, with the individual's part in the action predetermined, and the individual himself therefore irresponsible for the outcome. Instead he is perpetually at a cross-road; and though he likes to make decisions—it gives him a sense of power—he also shrinks from making them. His case is not too unlike that of the rat recently described by a psychologist: subjected to conditions involving more and more elaborate "multiple choice", the beast eventually became desperate, retreated into a complete psychosis—literally went mad from having to "choose" too often and under too complex conditions.

It is in part upon this sense of insecurity that our hypothesis about art rests. But "insecurity" must be taken from other standpoints as well. Many psychologists when they discuss it, describe it as an individual, even though very common phenomenon, and trace it to unfortunate experience or relationships early in life, generally associated with the mother or father. The poet Byron, to take a famous example, is thought to owe much of his instability and insecurity to his mother's extraordinarily erratic love for him and his nurse's ill treatment. There is no question that this kind of insecurity often enough appears. But it does so rather as a special and exaggerated case of the general situation of man than as a particular phenomenon. It is to that universal insecurity much more than to such special cases of it as Byron's that aesthetic experience is essentially related.

On this point many psychologists and, in fact, almost all writers who have been in any degree influenced by Freud, have gone astray in aesthetic theory. For their preoccupation with the abnormal in psychology has led them to ignore the implications, even though they may recognize the existence, of this universal and altogether normal sense of insecurity.

There is another situation equally universal in the lives

of individuals that must be considered at this point. It is the problem that faces every one from the mere physical fact of being born. The psychological significance of the experience of birth has entered into psychological theory, but we need not go into that here.[1] We might, however, try to realize fully one thing that being born means. It means the sudden removal from a completely homogeneous surrounding, the mother's womb, in which the infant's self is not really altogether distinguishable from the mother. This is, in fact, the single situation in life in which there is no "self and other", for self and other are continuous, homogeneous, and one. We do not suppose that this is a conscious experience of the infant. But it is certainly experience of some sort. Along with the pain and shock of birth there must come the sudden feeling of totally new surroundings: a temperature different from his own; textures—air, clothing; sounds; light. His sense awareness is not fully developed and he does not differentiate all these. But for the first time the boundaries of his physical person are marked off by something distinctly other than self. It may be pushing our argument too far to recall that, though a good laugh would serve the purpose of filling his lungs with air, what the infant utters at this point is a cry.

From the time of birth on through life, all experience and all knowledge are partial, not total; heterogeneous, not homogeneous. Adjustment to this is most difficult for the "higher" animal forms, and most of all difficult for man. For with the same break in physical continuity at birth the lower animal, because he inherits a more specialized set of instincts, has closer psychic continuity with

[1] The important work on this is by Otto Rank, *The Trauma of Birth*, London, 1929.

the past: he has less to learn "by his own efforts"; he may even be said to have brought much of his future experience with him into the world. Man, on the other hand, is more insecure in this situation. He has a wonderful instrument in his intelligence, but it is not easy to use and will not do everything for him. He still has instincts; but, as we have seen, most of these are instincts of need, and he has very few of the instincts for getting his needs filled. He can cry for food and he can suck; but of the more highly elaborated instincts such as are typified by the birds' sense of direction, he has few. This means that his primal instincts—the desire for self-preservation, and whatever other instincts he may be supposed to have—must work largely through his intelligence instead of through fixed inherited patterns. For all his powers, then, man is of all animals in certain ways the least at home with the external world when he first enters it. Yet he is so constituted that he must come to know it best.

From this point of view, all the activities of man beyond the mere preserving of his own life may be looked upon as so many ways of coping with the original problem of *self* and *other*. He is forever trying to break down the barrier; to make the difference between the self and the world outside once more non-existent; to conquer the partial, the scattered, the heterogeneous by the unity of art or religion or science; to absorb all things into himself by knowing them completely, or by possessing them. The scientist goes to work patiently, bit by bit, conquering fragments of knowledge though knowing that he will never understand one least thing completely.[1] He works

[1] *Cf.* S. Alexander: "Science arises from disappointment, hesitation and doubt." *Beauty and Other Forms of Value*, London, 1923, p. 193.

on, however, with a dim vision of an infinitely distant future time when someone like himself *will* know something completely and will therefore know everything: when, in other words, all will be one, complete knowledge being inconceivable except as meaning complete identity. But as he works he now and then makes his own little discoveries. And sometimes one of these so lights up the surrounding darkness that for a moment, in his excited recognition of a new truth, the pressure of all the unknown and all the partial things of life vanishes from him. Whether the truth is of any use to him or to the world does not matter. Whether it may even be proved false tomorrow does not matter at the moment. He has the thrilling but brief illusion of completeness, of knowing a whole. This is the aesthetic experience.

We have not thereby said that science is art. But the common notion that the scientist is in his way a poet too, has this much of truth.

The same kind of feeling is experienced by the religious mystic when he feels himself ecstatically united with God or the Universe. "Except a man shall say in his heart, I alone and God are in this world, he shall not find peace." So said the Abbot Allois in the Middle Ages. If the abbot's God was an extension and idealization of his self, as some modern thinkers contend, his achievement of the unity of all things is complete. For while he thinks *two* —"I alone and God"—he feels *one*. And so with the occasional systematic philosopher who believes that he has at last worked out an absolute and final theory of reality or has found the idea which is a key to infinite truth. In all these cases the momentary feeling of the discoverer as he contemplates his discovery, with no idea of its usefulness but so engrossed in the contemplation of its magnitude or its newness that his thought is what I must describe as *intensely arrested*, is focused with an extraordinarily strong focus upon the object itself—when this occurs and he feels himself to be imaginatively identified with the object, then the experience for him is identical with that of the artist in creative moments and with that of the inspired reader or audience. But there is an important difference. The mystic afterward accepts his experience not as illusion but intellectually as truth, as proof of man's intuitive power of making himself indeed one with the universe, or of his intuitive knowledge of God. His first thrilling pleasure will not recur unless he believes this. Another difference is perhaps even more significant. In science, in religion and philosophy, these aesthetic moments are incidental. They are not what the experiment was conducted for; they are not what the philosophical system or the religion was adopted for. These activities were all undertaken for practical purposes, to shape the external world, the "other", to our needs and desires either by knowledge or by faith. The work of art is not an attempt to control nature partially as far as we may by science, nor to control it mentally as we may do quite completely so long as we preserve an implicit faith in a comprehensive system, philosophical or religious. Art rather serves by suggestion or, as we shall find that to mean, by symbols, to let us feel *what the experience of complete control of a world-without would be like if it were possible*, while yet not attempting to influence our rational judgment by making us believe such control actually possible. It is pretty well agreed now that art is what we call disinterested. And much of what we mean by *disinterested* resides in this notion that art does not, in its essential quality as art, warp the judgment.

All life is full of experiences of this kind, some the most trivial, others profound, but many having the same central psychological value as art. A woman describes the pleasure of so planning meals, so contriving and adding and combining that all possible ends are served: the meals are excellent and varied, nothing is wasted, and now and then (almost the greatest of pleasure involved, though quite irrational) the refrigerator is completely emptied, everything is ended at once, and all may be started afresh. The satisfaction involved in this process goes quite beyond any of the useful purposes served. To the particular person of this illustration it does not in the least matter if some food is wasted. And no cook is much aided by an empty ice box. But the pleasure afforded by the fitting together of all these things for a single purpose is intensified by having become through some individual process of association a symbol of the universal problem successfully solved—unity found in variety, the many conquered by the one, the heterogeneous by the homogeneous, the world-without by the self. And so she finds an unusual and otherwise inexplicable pleasure in that activity which she herself has thought of as feeling "like the process of artistic creation".

Perhaps at this point I should explain the sense in which the term *symbol* is to be used, for it is a central part of what I shall have to say. The term is frequently made to carry a mystical content. Here it means nothing mystical or esoteric, though of course its complete definition waits upon the clarification of such other terms as *thought, knowledge,* and *emotion.* A symbol, however, here means merely anything which through association comes to suggest something other than itself so strongly that the suggested object rivals or overshadows in importance or vividness, *but without obliterating from consciousness,* the original object which is the symbol. The symbol and its meaning thus become fused in the imagination of the beholder. In this sense, such an activity as the preparation of food may be as much a symbol as any single or visible object.

A simpler illustration than the one we have just considered will take us even farther. A boy sits on a log and, as he talks, idly looks about for a small stick which he can fit into a nail hole. After several trials he finds one that just fits, and the discovery gives him a little glow of satisfaction, distinct but irrational. The whole incident is so trivial as not to interrupt his flow of conversation even for a moment; he had perhaps not even been clearly aware that he was looking for a stick or that he had seen the nail hole, until the small shock of pleasure brought his attention for a moment to what he had accomplished. This also was an aesthetic experience.

Anyone who has so much as heard of psychoanalysis, however, will at once see a sexual symbolism in this. Perhaps he will be right: its resemblance to primitive phallic ritual is obvious enough. A Freudian would probably see the same symbolism even in the preceding instance of the woman preparing food. But whether in the given experience of either the boy or the woman some sexual meaning was present or not, does not matter at all as far as the aesthetic problem is concerned, for it seems clear enough that the central value of each experience was something else. It is essential to realize here the different layers of meaning which a symbol may carry. The boy's action might, by psychoanalytical theory, symbolize also the process of nutrition, of filling himself with food; it might remind him unconsciously of his early experience of nursing. But it might also symbolize for him the perfect fitting of himself without conflict into the world; it might well have symbolized even purposefulness in the universe—the finding by apparent chance of that which seemed made and fitted precisely for a given end. But finally—and this is why we may call the experience an aesthetic one—it focuses into one simple and relatively comprehensible situation, a peg in a hole, a number of vaguely felt but important incomprehensibles. It forms a momentary synthesis of many related and yet different things. By being itself a symbol of one thing and another and another, the boy's action produces the momentary illusion that all things are one. And this is the chief function of the experience. It leads to no further action, it has no practical use, and it therefore permits the boy's mind to stop for an arrested moment without any suggestion of "you must do this about it" or "the result will be thus and so". The experience therefore seems complete in itself even though it symbolizes a great deal outside of itself. It is like a soap bubble in the air, complete, equidistant as it seems from all things without, not by its form leaning farther toward one thing than toward another, yet reflecting all the outside world upon its surface. This gives a psychic illusion of completeness which we know is impossible in actual life but which we are always unconsciously seeking through every means in our power.

The central value of the boy's and the woman's experience, then, resided not in any one of the meanings, but *in the fact of their fusion.* It is through failing to recognize this truth that psychoanalysis has lost its way in interpreting aesthetic experience. The Freudian school believes that the deepest of our repressions are those connected with sex because the sexual instinct has suffered more than other parts of our personality from social taboos. Freud's extreme emphasis on this has been criticized in recent years by other writers: it has been suggested that as a natural consequence of his profound discovery of the unconscious and its preoccupation with sex, Freud has seen sex as almost the whole psychological problem of man instead of only one problem among others. Without entering at length into the controversy, we might yet remind ourselves that the problem of existence itself is anterior to the problem of sex, that our growth by the division of cells is not sexual, and that the infant after birth does certainly have the problem of organizing his own self in relation not merely to his mother but to all external reality. The fundamental problems of life are all closely related in our experience, so that a suggestion of one of them will very likely carry with it a powerful suggestion of another. Jung and others have pointed out a close connection, for example, between sex and nutrition, hence between hunger and desire; so that sometimes one stands as a symbol in our minds for the other, sometimes a different experience will stand as a symbol for both.

Even this must complicate Freud's simple theory that art is the adult's version of the child's play, and that both are a working out in the fantasy of wish-fulfillment of certain repressed sexual desires originally connected with the parents and later associated with other persons of the opposite sex. Must we not rather see the artistic impulse as springing from the anterior and more general problem of existence, of which this problem of sex, important though it is, is only a part? Because sexual repression—now that it has been pointed out to us—is such a definite and relatively simple concept, many psychologists have been inclined to look upon the problem of the self and the world-without as an intellectual and derivative problem, or as a speculative problem without the deep emotional urgency of the other. It is more than conceivable, however—it seems in fact most likely—that when primitive man uses sexual symbols in his cosmogony he may be applying his concept of sex to the solving of his universal problem, rather than inventing a cosmogony in order to sublimate his sexual desire. The problem of sex is more concrete and so more easily identified, but it is not therefore more urgent than the problem of "self and other".

To put into something like a definition, then, a conception of aesthetic experience which differs from those current among psychologists but which I think is not in conflict with any of the sounder tenets of modern psychology, we may say that aesthetic pleasure arises when a circumstance or combination of circumstances so operates upon our mind as to become for us a symbol—imaginative but not logical, perhaps illusory but not deceptive—of that fundamental synthesis which we long for, the synthesis of the self and the world-without, and when this symbolic value so takes possession of our mind as to overshadow, even though but momentarily, any other value the circumstance may possess.

CHAPTER THREE

"NATURAL BEAUTY"

Thus far we have discussed none of the kinds of experience which the world at large is accustomed to call aesthetic, and these we must now consider. Of them all, apart from the arts, the most commonly recognized as a source of pleasure is probably nature or "the beauty of nature". Not all writers, but most, agree that the delight experienced in the presence of some natural scenes is of essentially the same kind as that produced by great art. Here we have a problem immeasurably more complex than that of the boy with his peg and hole, for in his case any value that the incident might have would be a symbolic value; it could not conceivably have had any other.[1] In the pleasures of nature a great many things inevitably become mixed up with the aesthetic and the symbolic, and we cannot even pretend to disentangle them all. Some, however, may be distinguished.

Let us take, for example, a typical city dweller of the upper middle classes who knows the country pretty well and is accustomed to spend his summer vacations there. Any sunny day in the country is likely to give him cer-

---

[1] It should perhaps be remarked here again that this experience is not an important one. The pleasure afforded, in spite of the magnitude of all that the symbol represented, was but barely noticeable. Of the reason for this, more will be said later.

tain pleasures. He has the physical comfort of the sun shining on his skin and opening his pores, and of breathing air unpolluted by city smoke or gasoline fumes; he has the mental satisfaction of thinking how good it is for him or what a pleasing tan he will acquire. He is also free from the responsibilities of his work and is away from surroundings which would remind him of work. Instead, his surroundings by the reminder of former summers fill his mind with vague images and recollections of past periods of freedom, perhaps of past irresponsible summer flirtations, of past youthful pleasure in country life, of pleasant games or successful shots at golf. And so on. Altogether, he is in a state of satisfaction, and he bestows this satisfaction lavishly on the scene about him. It's a fine day; there's a fine oak tree; it looks as if there will be fine crops, which will mean prosperity for the farmers and so more or less for everybody, including himself. Now this is a very pleasant, expansive state of mind; but it is not what we mean by an aesthetic experience. For in this mood the varying elements are not focused at any single point in such a way as to present a symbol for a deeper or more urgently desired unification.

And yet practically the same situation may produce an aesthetic response. The sun, let us suppose, breaks out from a cloud and floods the landscape with light. Suddenly everything becomes sharply differentiated: contrasts are acute; the light is brilliant, the shadow is black; even the minute details of the scene, single leaves and edges of stone, present extremes of bright and dark not apparent before. The eye roams over it all and the mind becomes conscious of all this exhibition of difference brought about by the single power of the sun; the extremes of opposites have, for the imagination at this moment, unity as their cause; or the sameness of the light-and-dark contrast everywhere visible, lends to contrast itself a kind of unity, so that again a symbol is found for the dissolving of the many into the one. Other things enter into the experience, of course. Probably the excitement is increased by the physically stimulating or irritating effect of bright dancing light upon the eyeballs. And the sudden warmth of sunlight has probably stimulated the circulation of blood and increased the pulse rate. These and innumerable other things no doubt add to or take away from the intensity of experience, but its special and peculiar character is recognizable through all the varying degrees of intensity.

At this point we can no longer avoid mention of that oldest and most insoluble question: Does the "beauty" reside in the object or in the mind of the beholder? Is this second scene that I have described beautiful in itself (and the first one not beautiful) regardless of whether the beholder actually experienced an aesthetic feeling or not? I am no more able to answer this question than any of the great philosophers have been, and it will rise again to plague us when we come to discuss standards of taste in the arts. Here I can only say provisionally that I arbitrarily define beauty as that which produces or tends to produce in the beholder, under favorable conditions of mood and attention, an aesthetic response.

Sometimes the external means by which the imaginative unification is brought about can be—at least in part—isolated by analysis, and sometimes they cannot. Often the features of a scene that combine into a symbol are so many and so subtle that no conscious analysis is fine enough to discover them. When this is so, we can only assume that the process is the same because it "seems" the same. And there are enough simple or partially analyzable cases to give us confidence in the principle, though even in these we are sure that many unobserved circumstances contribute to the effect.

One or two aspects of natural scenery that commonly produce in the beholder an aesthetic response may illustrate this further. The outline of familiar hills or mountains seen at twilight, clearly defined against the sky, almost invariably seems beautiful to us. This is probably because, though we already know something of the infinite complexities of form and color that normally intervene between ourselves and that distant outline and these are dimly present to our consciousness, yet now all that is exposed to our actual sight is the simplified outline of the hills—external reality thus suddenly reduced to a single curved line such as we might almost ourselves draw with a pencil. And again this becomes a symbol which satisfies our desire to simplify all things to one. There is even sometimes a further suggestion for the beholder of the scene. This, he feels, is truth—the true shape of earth itself, with all "accidents" of color and detail made invisible. It is not, of course, actually any truer reality than the full daytime scene; but the removal of trees from his sight, bringing to his attention so powerfully the shape of the mountain itself, simplifies reality into something that he feels for the moment that he understands; and again he is relieved from the teasing of partial, fragmentary knowledge and experience, and enjoys a feeling of completeness.

This seems true. And yet we are reminded of something quite contrary that we have always believed in, the charm of mystery. We have just now been describing aesthetic pleasure as if it were the pleasure of knowledge or of the imagined feeling of knowledge. But do we not also have a pleasure in *not* knowing? Watching mountains against the horizon at twilight almost always brings to the surface of consciousness a sense of the mysterious which is an integral part of our pleasure. In the face of this common fact, may we still suppose the universal foundation of the aesthetic to be man's desire to know all things? The answer remains, I think, that we can. For if we recall distinctly the elements of the mood described, I think we find a certain pain or sadness always mingling with the pleasure we enjoy in contemplation of the mysterious. The unknown, lending that tinge of sadness to our mood, is present to our mind; but instead of rejecting it, we accept it as something that, "after all", we can live with. In ordinary life, we suppress from our conscious minds any distinct thought of all the unknown that we are not engaged at the moment in trying to solve or to chisel bits from. But at such a moment as I have described, where twilight simplifies lines and unifies by the draining or dimming of color all the visible scene, it is as if so much is known to us, so much unity accomplished, that we can endure the awareness of much that cannot be known. And so we are filled with that pleasurable sadness, the "sweet melancholy" of the poets that is familiar to everyone. Ordinarily we do not let ourselves feel consciously this mystery of our life in the external world because to do so would overwhelm us. But at these moments the pleasure of the aesthetic unification makes the eternal mystery a gentler experience, and the mere relief of letting its tide flow into our conscious mind from the depths in which it is usually concealed, gives us pleasure in the very sadness. This is a common experience. It constitutes, incidentally, much of what we mean in criticism when we use the term Romantic, though this feeling was not invented, with the term, in the eighteenth century. Leonardo records something of it in a notebook: "Consider in the streets at nightfall the faces of men and women when it is bad weather, what grace and sweetness they manifest!" Literature and the arts are full of it.

These illustrations have been general ones—cases in which, given a receptive mood, most people would have an aesthetic experience of some degree of intensity. But there are other situations or combinations of phenomena in nature which perhaps for only one individual would take on aesthetic significance, and we shall have to stop for one illustration of this kind.

On a bright, crisp spring day, before leaves were fully out, a man was overlooking from a height the bend in a creek where breeze ruffled the water. The shifting glitter of its water formed the natural focus of the scene, for a physiological if for no other reason; for the waves were small and sharp from the erratic gusts and so caught the sunlight in many confused points of brilliance. These in turn were echoed less sharply by the glitter of sunlight upon fresh opening leaves; the eyes were further stimulated by a bright sky, and the body by the slightly sharp air alternating with moments of warmth when the breeze fell. Into this scene then entered one trivial but very unusual phenomenon, the effect of which was to focus everything at the moment into intense unity of aesthetic experience for the beholder. Far below the cliff in a quiet stretch of water a long snake appeared swimming toward the opposite shore. It was clearly visible, though at a remarkable distance, and its head and tail were pointed as it swam by the most brilliant sparkle in all the scene.

The impression of all this upon the beholder was very strong, and he was later able to disentangle by analysis a good many of the symbolic meanings and formal relationships that he had been aware of. The obvious meaning that this suggests to a psychologist, once more, is a sexual one, for snakes are one of the traditional sexual symbols. This meaning he was not aware of, though he would not attempt to prove that it was absent. The other meanings, those which he recognized, were all likeness-contrast ones. The snake's movement was slow and steady, that of the wind-swept water quick and erratic. The snake was the single animal in a world of vegetable. And while elsewhere the cause of the glitter—the wind— was invisible, there the creature was the cause made visible of the most brilliant isolated sparkles. All these contrasts were drawn together into unity by the continuous brilliance everywhere, ranging from the slightest to the most intense. And finally the effect of the whole was magnified by surprise. For the snake was seen at such a distance as one would have supposed to be impossible, and the beholder had therefore the illusion of something almost supernatural, "as if" he were granted in the form of a water snake magical insight into the unifying cause of outward things.

In analyzing the aesthetic experience into symbols of this kind, it is essential to realize clearly that the suggestion of the symbol operates upon the feeling side of our nature, not on the intellectual. We do not, that is, consciously formulate a thought that, as light and shade are produced by the single sun, so all multiple things in life may be seen as one.

Modern philosophy and psychology are in such an unsatisfactory state at present in the matter of definitions of *intellect* and *emotion*, that it does not seem profitable to go into that question here. And since we all have a more or less similar practical way of using the terms, their general popular sense will suffice for us. It does not even seem important at this point to ask whether we should postulate a separate and distinct "aesthetic emotion", parallel with other emotions like fear, love, hate. All that we need be sure of is that there is a recognizable and distinct kind of experience that we call aesthetic; that the peculiar character of this experience derives from *feeling* rather than from *thinking*; and that this is true in spite of the almost universal tendency to identify "beauty" with "truth". It further seems most probable that such elements as we have here been describing in particular cases are the kind of elements that universally constitute the aesthetic experience, and that they are used by the mind unconsciously to represent a oneness of the self and the world-without which the mind is always desiring.

Besides this unity and, indeed, in consequence of it, the aesthetic experience is further characterized by being a state of the self in which no will is involved. Will may have been exercised in achieving the experience, and may exert itself by fits and starts in recapturing the moments of appreciation; but the moment itself of aesthetic appreciation is like the mystic's moment of exaltation, willless. Indeed, in this respect religion, love, art, and the great moments of science are alike. The fact I think will be recognized as true, even though we are aware too that within the aesthetic state are often born the seeds of new achievement—stimulation or inspiration to further uses of the will.

This will-lessness is perhaps why the image of a globe or circle is so often used to describe aesthetic experience.

The "perfectly rounded form" of a song or a poem, the "microcosm", "completing the full circle": such phrases suggest the one geometrical shape that *does not go anywhere* outside itself, that points no direction but, instead, represents a balance of forces that leaves nothing for the will to accomplish—until the shape begins to fail, the bubble to break, the drop to elongate. Then the will is called forth again: a direction is once more suggested.

It is necessary to return here to our earlier discussion of the origin of man's aesthetic impulse. The attribution of this to (to put it crudely) the unsatisfactory difference between existence after birth and existence before will encounter two very serious objections. It will be urged, in the first place, that such a theory presupposes a degree of consciousness and sensitivity, and a power of memory on the part of the newly born, and even the unborn infant which its organism does not possess. But this, I think, is a hasty conclusion; for it is not necessary to postulate what we commonly understand as memory or consciousness on the part of the unborn infant. We need assume hardly more than what we now know to be the very rudimentary "teachableness" of a primitive single-celled amoeba. Even in this lowest member of the animal world, with its relatively undifferentiated structure, we see present action influenced by past experience. Perhaps an example will make this clear.

In a well-known zoological experiment an amoeba was placed in a glass tube of water of normal temperature. Beyond a bend in the tube hot water was inserted, and at the same time a ray of light, to which the amoeba is naturally attracted, was thrown upon the tube at the point where the hot water began. The amoeba immediately moved into the beam of light; then, finding the water hot, moved back. At first, each time the light appeared, the amoeba swam to it. But after a number of such experiences, finding the light always accompanied by excessive heat, it ceased to pursue the light at all, and continued to remain in its original end of the tube even though the hot water was removed. In other words, something that looks to us like an association-of-ideas connection between two experiences came to have an influence upon the amoeba's way of life. The amoeba cannot be said to have had a memory or to have made a judgment about heat and light. But the repeated contact had some lasting effect upon its organism and influenced its subsequent actions. Hardly more than this need be postulated in the case of the human infant: only that the predominantly homogeneous character of its prenatal life should have some pervasive influence in limiting or controlling in some respects its post-natal manner of behaving. In this sense, it seems to us, prenatal experience can scarcely be imagined *not* to have a profound effect upon the general organism of the infant, upon its impulses to action and consequently upon its emotions. We need presuppose in the newborn child no distinct memory in order to suppose this much, nor any highly differentiated sense perceptions.

We may, in fact, be justified in going much further. Ancient philosophers and modern psychologists are pretty much at one in telling us that we can have no conception of anything of which we have had no experience. This is one reason why the old theory about innate ideas of the existence of God, for example, was sometimes bolstered by supposing the soul to have known God before birth. The idea turns up in literature as recently as in Wordsworth's *Ode on Intimations of*

Immortality.[1] Now the concept of unity is one of the most deeply pervasive and influential in all our existence. Even in polytheistic religions we see clearly the struggle for it. One god will be the king of the gods; or one race of gods, under its king, will overthrow the earlier race: always there is apparent the symbolized struggle for conquest of many by one. All knowledge, of course, is based upon the same constitution of our minds, our preference for order and system instead of chaos. It satisfies us, for instance, to find a point of view from which the apple and rose can be related as of one botanical family instead of two, or to find a formula—that is, a point of view— which gives a seeming identity to the falling of an apple and the movement of the planets. This unifying habit of our minds is indeed too well recognized by philosophers and too pervasive in everyday experience to require elaboration or illustration here.

Whether this unifying character is an attribute of reality itself we have no certain means of knowing, though religion and science both presume it. What we do know with certainty is its dominant place in the constitution of the human mind. And it is at least easily conceivable that such a constitution is the psychic outcome of the development, through biological change, of a "conscious" type of organism with its reduced instinctual knowledge and its increased intelligence, together with the effect upon that type of organism of the universal experience of birth into the world.

I have been claiming more in the way of a psychological theory here than is needed for our discussion of aesthetics, and there is certainly no need to urge the ac-

[1] Wordsworth did not commit himself to a belief in this, but he derived the idea from those who did.

ceptance of it all. But I have wanted to provide a brief background, some at least of which will seem both pertinent and acceptable, to relate our notion of the aesthetic to other aspects of life. The view of aesthetics presented here does, however, require that we accept these things as true: that life is not altogether satisfactory to man; that he has only the remotest chance, if any, of ever making it entirely satisfactory; and that one of his most fundamentally disturbing problems—disturbing through the biological necessity of his difference from the "lower" animals, however this difference may have come about— is his desire for unity, when faced with the multiplicity and otherness of the world.

Before turning to the next phase of our subject, which is art, one other objection, however, must be met. It is this: that what has been said about the effect of birth with its change, presumably by pain, from the homogeneous to the heterogeneous in surroundings, is too negative; that if the experience were as we say, man's dominant impulse would be a regressive one—a refusal to accept the world outside, a desire to go back where he came from, or an impulse toward death. And this obviously is not the way he behaves. If it were, a child would perhaps refrain from taking its first breath, would certainly never grow up, and if by any chance he did so, his whole "civilization" would no doubt be rather like an animal's period of hibernation; he would seek the warmest, snuggest, darkest spot in the tropics and sleep away his life. Something, clearly, prevents his doing this. Whether we call it the will to live or the instinct for self-preservation, or something about his charged atoms that makes them stick together and resist disintegration, at any rate he has a positive impulse to stay in the world and do something with it. If he does not die out of un-willingness to live by himself and by his own efforts, it means that he has somehow come to terms with life. It means that he can find positive values in his new world while he is yet homesick for his old one. This is true even though he spends his life trying to unite the new and the old world, even though what he does with life is to try to take in or control more and more of the in-numerable aspects of reality until some day, at the un-imaginable end of an infinitely long time, he or his kind will again reach the complete synthesis of all that is: all will be related, all will be one, he and his surroundings will be identical. Only, from the time that he first en-counters the external world, the longed-for unity of all things has to be sought *through* and *by including* that world and cannot be found by avoiding it. Multiplicity having once smitten him, he must and will hunt it down. So his strongest impulse is to go out and meet the world, but in meeting it to shape it with all his faculties, as far as he may, into the form of experience that has already shaped him.

That is the active life; but, as we have already said, in this he can never achieve complete success. The pressure of his awareness of this he relieves in various ways, by adopting a system—scientific, philosophical, or religious— by giving to his sexual life more than its mere animal function, by providing himself with the imaginative uni-fications of aesthetic experience.

CHAPTER FOUR

ART ORGANIZED

THE test of any definition or analysis of the aesthetic
motive must lie finally, not in its application to such
experiences as I have hitherto described, but in its application to the recognized forms of art. It may be readily
granted that men do have those other experiences and
that they are often associated with the enjoyment of
"beauty", and yet it might still be contended that the
central function of art is something else. Have we been
too arbitrary in appropriating the term *aesthetic* for this
particular kind of experience, recognizable and common
and otherwise unnamed though it may be?

Certainly this experience is not the whole of art. For
the arts are elaborate, highly organized forms of human
activity. They do not occur by chance. They not only
give man satisfaction, by presenting to him unified objects for will-less contemplation; they also make demands, for they require the exertion of will in attaining
them. Moreover, they obviously have important social
values as well as values to the individual. We are therefore obliged to consider whether our postulate—that the
central, or original, or characteristic mark of the aesthetic
that sets it off as a whole from other forms of experience
is the imaginative symbolic unification of actually or ap-

parently non-unified reality—whether this postulate will survive an analytical study of the arts, in terms either of their values or of their various conventions and forms and content. A complete study of this kind lies beyond the province of this work and beyond my own powers; but a few threads may be followed here, a few questions raised and some answers tentatively offered. Throughout the discussion, however, this modifying supposition will have to be borne in mind: that the desire to unify reality in imagination—being not essential to the preservation of life, and being, moreover, in the evolutionary sense a modern development, a concomitant of growing self-consciousness—is often not a consciously recognized motive of action and is therefore quite likely to be confused with and even overshadowed by other motives or impulses; that the artist, consequently, is likely to wander into other pastures than his characteristic one and to build up other besides the purely aesthetic values, without our being always clearly aware of the difference.

The first question arises from the fact that art is so obviously, in some respects, a *social* phenomenon. This aspect of art has, as everyone knows, been stressed in recent years, especially by social historians and anthropologists, who tend to regard social usefulness as the prime reason for the existence of art. On the other hand, the experience that I have described as aesthetic is purely personal and individual, shared often by no one and certainly not requiring to be shared. This we can continue to regard as the basis of art only if we can assure ourselves that the socialization of such an experience would not necessarily conflict with its original purpose or destroy its effect. Actually, I think that we can be assured of this and of more besides; for I think we may find that the social organization of aesthetic activity not only does not destroy its value to the individual or its character as an individual experience, but that it even enhances that value in various ways.

In the first place, by organizing the aesthetic into the arts we have brought aesthetic experience more within our control than it could otherwise be: we have made its effects more certain, sometimes more "pure", often more intense, and always more re-capturable. The aesthetic experience that comes to us by chance or from sources not specifically organized for an aesthetic purpose is likely to be occasional, fleeting, and incomplete. In any scene of nature, however "beautiful" it may be, there are almost innumerable elements which cannot be used by the mind to secure a unified effect. The mind, in such a case, constructs its own unity out of certain elements of the scene, disregarding the rest. As Santayana has said, every landscape "to be seen has to be composed"; and the composing will be done by every individual mind differently. This is also true of a work of art: here too the beholder constructs his own picture out of the painted one. But his construction is far more controlled or guided by the artist. Consequently, if the beholder is at home in the idiom of painting, the aesthetic effect upon him of a picture is almost certain to be more complete and more easily repeatable at will than is possible for aesthetic experience outside the arts.

But non-artistic aesthetic experience is less within our control by reason of still another fact. In order to experience beauty, the suggestive symbol and one's receptive mood must coincide. Without some mental predisposition at the moment, imagination will not make use of the proffered symbols; for here "the ripeness is all". This is more true of the enjoyment of beauty than of most things in life. Our will is active most of the time, active in trying to satisfy our wants in one way or another. And this self-interested activity of will is a block to the aesthetic mood. By organizing aesthetic experience into the arts, however, we gain control—something less than perfect—of its comings and goings. The arts serve as churches or temples which we enter for a predetermined purpose. And just as the quiet of church, the light—all the physical surroundings, in fact—through the power of long association tend to draw the worshiper into a religious mood, so the mere leafing through a book; the entering of a building in which one expects to receive an aesthetic impression; the sight of colored rectangles upon a wall; the sound of musicians tuning; the rise of a curtain; if one is a painter, the very smell of paints and turpentine—anything, in fact, which is associated with organized art serves a kind of preparatory aesthetic purpose, serves to free the mind of personal and interested preoccupations and to detach the will from its usual aims. Thus, by being fixed to a given spot—chained, that is, to a set of conventions, or expressed in expected mediums which can be either repeated or revisited—the sets of relations which may produce an aesthetic effect will most often do so successfully. On the other hand, beauty deprived of all conventional aid of this kind suffers in its power to be effective as a preacher does who tries for converts by speaking to casual passers-by on a street corner. He has to compete with too much that is immediate; and for one person who will be startled into accepting his message, hundreds will pass by with indifference or contempt who, if they had gone to church to hear him, might have listened with pious feelings. Entirely unconventional art, if such a thing could be, would have this weakness not only for the audience but even for the creator: he himself without the aid of convention [1] would have difficulty in recapturing the mood in which his creation originated, and this might prevent his completing a work of art, or hinder his pleasure in it afterward.

On the other hand, there are also certain areas outside the arts that have been subjected in a degree to this same convention which sets up a kind of pre-aesthetic mood by making us know what we are expected to feel, and which have therefore fallen into almost the same category as art itself in some respects. The "beauty of nature", for instance, especially since the romantic period in western culture, is such a convention. We are accustomed to expect almost automatically to feel an aesthetic pleasure in "fine" natural scenery. So, unless something urgent intervenes, we are apt to fall into a receptive mood beforehand. Undoubtedly, more of genuinely aesthetic pleasure has been obtained from nature since, say, 1760, than was felt before, though nature itself is no more "beautiful" and man himself probably no more sensitive to aesthetic experience. There are no doubt quite as many persons now as in the seventeenth century who if entirely untouched by convention would sometimes be in the mood to describe the Alps with John Evelyn as "the rubbish of the earth". But the convention that now associates mountains with beauty or the "sublime", while it renders some of us hypocritical and others of us rebellious, most often operates to fill our mind in

---

[1] In the term *convention*, of course, are included less extrinsic things than physical surroundings: the mediums, the various forms of the arts are also what we mean by conventions.

advance with poetic or picturesque associations, and thus make us ready for an aesthetic experience.

In tracing these purely individual and aesthetic advantages in the social organization of the arts, we need not insist that it was primarily to obtain these advantages that art came to be organized. Organization may have arisen—to put some of the commonest anthropological theories crudely—as a means of impressing the group ideology upon individuals; or as a means either of controlling or of strengthening, in the interests of society, the individual sexual impulse; or as a means of sharing or intensifying religious enthusiasm. I myself do not think that the origin of art lies in any of these things. Nor have students of primitive art proved any such theories yet. But even should they succeed in proving them, it would hardly matter to our present argument. For even then these social values could not be considered as definitely constitutive of art, since they do not serve to differentiate it from the teachings of morality or from any other form of social pressure. All that could be proved would be that for the purposes of social organization man has seized upon some obscure but powerful pleasure-impulse in his individual nature which can be exploited as a means of social control. And there would remain the problem of discovering what that impulse is, that can be so used.

We may continue to regard art, then, in spite of anthropologists or utilitarians, as the characteristic vehicle for the aesthetic impulse, however we define that impulse, so long as we can see that there are important ways in which the institutions of art have been favorable to individual aesthetic values, and that the direction taken by the evolution of art is such a direction as would naturally further the purpose of the aesthetic, let it have whatever social values it may besides.

But this raises another question, one that has already been hinted at. If the aesthetic experience is essentially one of individual rather than social psychology, what significance shall we see in the social relationship that is invariably present in the practice and enjoyment of art, in consequence of the bare and obvious fact that art (as distinct from non-artistic aesthetic experience) is always a *shared* activity? There is always a relationship between creator and observer, or between members in a group of performers. In painting, for example, the beholder is always aware of some degree of contact with the creator of the picture. Sometimes the painter's life or character and his other work will be present in the mind of the beholder. Or, if he is looking at the production of a quite unknown artist, even here at the most impersonal he will be aware that through the picture he is sharing in the mind of another human being: that this very object at which he is gazing, with all its power to evoke responses in himself, is the production of another human mind like his own. And so through all the avenues of art. The older the work—provided it still evokes a response in us—the more profoundly we feel a sense of unity in man, not only between the painter or poet and ourself, but among all the actual or potential sharers in it, men past and to come. Admiration, companionship, social solidarity may all be a part of it.

This kind of value is often taken as proof that art has primarily a social purpose and origin. But even this, as may be observed I think by anyone who analyzes his own response to a work of art, even this "social" value of human sharing in an art work, becomes absorbed by and is part of the aesthetic feeling itself. If the general experience of art, that is, may be described as a feeling that so many things, or such unexpected and different things are seen at the moment, through a symbol, to be united, that "it is as if" all things were one—then the observer's impression that he shares the very experience of the artist and of all sensitive observers who may behold the same painting, brings one more element into the imaginative unity of the picture. Not only, in a still life by a great painter, do we feel kettle, table, fruit, and dead fish to be so united by color and form that they symbolize a deeper unity of all reality; the power of the symbol is strengthened by our feeling that through it the human race also is united—the artist with the beholder, and the beholders with each other, through times past and to come. The potentially universal imaginative sharing of any work of art, in other words, is like an additional element of subject matter in the picture, which becomes unified along with the other elements.

What we have said up to this point about the social aspect of art and, before that, about primary differences between organized art and unorganized aesthetic experience, may appear too obvious to need saying: we may seem to be reciting A B C's as if they were literature. The trouble is, however, that we do not generally realize these things vividly enough to see some of their implications. By failing to reconcile with each other the individual aesthetic and the social values of art, or by failing to take account of the original character of non-artistic aesthetic experience, we make for ourselves problems in aesthetics that need not be. Critics, for instance—and not only critics but many others of us—have viewed with concern and some suspicion the pleasure that we all derive from the accidents of age in a work of art. What mere time and human use have done should not, they feel, affect aesthetic value. Hence it is thought to be a false sense of values or else sentimentality that makes us take added pleasure in the worn stair-treads of an ancient building, in its mossy, time-eaten stones, in the imperfect and worn surface of an old statue, in the faded or time-darkened colors of a painting. Our pleasure in these things, even if real, is not purely aesthetic, it is felt: for the true lover of art should take pleasure only in the thing in itself, the exact object as the artist created it. —So the artistic purists protest. And yet we, and they also as a rule, continue to be moved by this suggestion of age and of the continuity of man that has become a visible part of a work of art, though we suffer a little in our aesthetic consciences for our pleasure.

Our sense of guilt, however, may disappear if we recall that in non-artistic experience of beauty the beholder through selection creates out of any elements that may be present his own symbols of unification, and that even in art the artist only partially controls and guides it for him; that the experience itself grows out of the individual need for imaginative unification of reality, and that the need is filled partly by his way of looking at the object. If the same symbol, through inevitable changes in its face, comes to unify more elements of reality than the artist intended, there is no aesthetic loss, but only gain; and there is no necessary conflict between the "inherent" and the "sentimental" values of an art work: both, since the viewpoint is the beholder's, form part of the same imaginative symbol.

While we are glancing at the relation between social and aesthetic functions of art it may be well to examine briefly one of the theories of aesthetic motive often held today. We shall have to consider it because of its evident truth in certain respects and because, if sustained as a complete hypothesis, it involves a violent contradiction of the views here presented. The theory is that artistic creation originates in the desire for immortality on the part of the creator. This idea is peculiarly appealing today because it fits very well into the psychoanalytic view of art as a sublimation of sexual desire, and at the same time is consistent with modern anthropological studies which bring out clearly the relation between art and religion among primitive peoples. In early non-individual cultures, it is supposed, art is the product of the group immortalizing itself as a group. As the individual self-consciousness develops in more modern cultures, this impulse also becomes individualized in the artist: he begins to sign his name to his productions, to mark them by his own individual style, to think of fame; and the group then finds its immortality only vicariously through him as their representative.

This is a beguiling theory; in some respects it almost rings true. It provides, moreover, a beguiling parallel to the psychological aspects of physical reproduction, in the desire for continued existence of the self through children. And it can be reinforced by almost endless citations from artists themselves. The language in which artistic creation is described frequently becomes altogether obstetrical: the pangs and throes of birth, the love and protection of one's "brain-child" or the "child of one's imagination"—such images almost always appear in accounts of the creative process. There can be little doubt that these phrases represent more than merely the analogy between two ways of bringing into existence something which had never been before; they almost certainly do represent a feeling on the part of the creator that he has produced an extension of himself which may live on after him.

The specific desire for fame too is a commonplace among artists: Keats's *I think I shall be among the English Poets after my death* is but one of many expressions of this, and its importance to the artist is not to be lessened by recalling that in the same month in which Keats said this in a letter he also wrote: "I feel assured I should write from the mere yearning and fondness I have for the Beautiful even if my night's labours should be burnt every morning and no eye ever shine upon them." But this last statement of Keats is no more to be ignored than the former one, and it also has many parallels both in the sayings of artists and in common experience. For who has not drawn pictures and built houses in the sand where the tide will wash them? The truth seems usually to be that the artist would like fame but that he would create anyhow.

Desire for immortality is a deep and universal desire, intimately bound up with all our other deepest impulses by threads which we need not attempt here to trace. Like other strong impulses, it will find an outlet wherever it can. And artistic creation is a very good outlet for it. There can be little question that the desire to immortalize the self furnishes much of the energy required for artistic creation. But there are many reasons besides the denial of artists themselves—who are in the best position to know by introspection but who also can scarcely avoid bias and self-justification in analyzing their own motives—there are many other reasons for not accepting this impulse as the primary aesthetic one.

First of all, this motive fails to account for the particular, the highly special forms that art has taken. The universal importance of form in art, the use of limited, highly specialized mediums, often not of the most permanent substance—these do not strike us as the inevitable choice for vehicles of self-perpetuation. Apart from other obvious ways of seeking fame—the way of a Caesar, or of an inventor if his motive too is considered to be that of fame—we can fancy many more direct traps for the attention of posterity than some, at least, of the arts—than dancing, for instance, and the interpretive arts in music and the theater where the creation inevitably dies with the creator or before him.[1] And we should expect the other arts to have taken a more directly autobiographical turn than they have done: for it would be stretching definitions considerably to contend that a painting, however impressionistic or personal in manner, of lemons, grapes, and a wine bottle, is as natural a means for self-immortalization as a self-portrait would be. Occasional bits of evidence from the lives of artists also— from their actions, that is, and not only from their words —tend somewhat to damage the immortality theory. Many painters, for example, lose interest in their work once it is finished. And many authors never re-read their own books. Bach was notoriously careless about the preservation of his manuscripts. And although such evidence as this can be explained away—a sense of guilt, for example, might be postulated to account for an artist's destruction of his brain-children—the mere fact that it requires a good deal of explaining is in itself some evidence against the theory.

But there are two other almost insuperable objections

[1] Is it necessary to defend the notion of the interpreter as an artist?

to it. The first is that it allows no place for the admittedly aesthetic character of some non-artistic experience, particularly in the response to the "beauty of nature". Self-immortalization cannot easily be identified with this, and yet there are few thinkers who exclude nature altogether from the realm of the aesthetic. The second objection is that such a theory when applied to any except the most communal forms of art does not sufficiently take account of the audience. The artist, it has been said, achieves immortality himself, and his audience achieves it through identification with him. But actually only the group itself can confer immortality upon the artist: his fugue is immortal only if it is preserved and played and heard. And his listeners preserve him only if he gives them something that they value. The group does not deify a member just because he desires deification. And if we ask what they do deify him for, the only answer is, "For his fugue." So we are back where we started.

In the actual process of artistic creation, by the overwhelming weight of evidence we gather that the artist is not thinking about what his public desires; he is composing for himself, for his own ear.[1] If, then, his aim is immortality, which he achieves only through the will of the group, what is he doing, and what is he doing it for, when he is writing for himself? The immortality theory thus appears to be begging a considerable part at least of its question.

Although the desire for immortality cannot be thought of as the differentia distinguishing art from other human activities, it can be seen to play its part here as elsewhere, working often, though not always, in harmony with the aesthetic aim. Without its stimulus, the artist might find

[1] For the discussion of this the reader is referred to page 61 hereafter.

his labor too heavy: he might often half satisfy himself with visionary creation rather than subject himself to the test of actualizing it. For the artist's work is not easy: it is, in fact, one of the most difficult of human activities. Nor is it as a rule well rewarded in any practical terms. Its success is never sure. Its end is, if looked at unsympathetically, "a mere symbol". Yet an artist will devote his whole life to it at a sacrifice of other more profitable forms of achievement. And, mere symbol that it is, it is highly valued by mankind; if it is "great" art the symbolic value will be lasting and will bring fame or immortality to the artist. This possibility plays its part, then, in greater or less degree with each artist, by adding, perhaps immeasurably, to the energy and persistence with which he pursues his aims. His desire for immortality may even influence his choice of subject or of idiom. "This", he may think suddenly, seeing another man's experiment, visions of achievement and perpetual fame floating before him, "this is a fine promising field. I must get into it." And he may yet be a good and sincere artist. So far goes the impulse toward self-immortalization in the creation of art, and no farther. What this impulse does not have anything to do with, is the determination of what makes all art to be art (rather than science, history, or anything else); it does not, that is, determine *the kind of activity that art shall be.* This is determined by the "aesthetic" motive.

Having given even this much place in artistic creation to a non-aesthetic element, however, we shall have to restate and modify a generalization made in an earlier chapter and at that time made broadly for the sake of simplicity. We said that in the aesthetic experience there is no element of will involved, that the feeling of the will's being at rest is, in fact, one of the most recognizable and one of the most important features of the experience. Yet we must by now have seen that the exercise of will to secure this will-less end is a very large part of what we call artistic activity, whether creative or appreciative. And in actual experience the presence of will and the absence of it are always interwoven moment by moment. We work to understand a picture, or to produce it; we see the vision for a moment and then lose it, catch another fragment of it, work to fit them together, finally see the whole, even then perhaps lose it, work for it again, and next time find it a slightly different whole. Thus what we described originally as a simple and single experience is rarely that in actual life. We cannot even say that in artistic creation the will is exerted constantly during the creation of a work, and then laid to rest in enjoyment of the result. The whole process is more fluid than this, or more shifting. Nevertheless, its characteristic tone or flavor is given to it by those momentary feelings of will-less synthesis. Without them, no experience would have the recognizable character of the aesthetic; on the other hand, though these moments rarely occur without the aid of the will, they sometimes do—or so nearly without the aid of will that we are not aware of its exercise.

This activity of will to produce an aesthetic result, however, comes to have a distinct value of its own as a by-product of its chief function. It has value—for the artist in a very great degree and for the audience in a slighter—not only because it produces a desired aesthetic result but also because, like any other exercise of the will, it satisfies the need for achievement; gives him a pleasant sense of power from the mere fact that he is successfully exercising his will, regardless of the importance to him of the end. The satisfaction of the ego in achievement and the desire for immortality which we have been discussing—the two intimately bound up with each other—both play a great part in artistic production, then; but their part is really incidental and not intrinsic, a consequence of the inevitable interrelation of all the fundamental aspects of life, and not in themselves constitutively essential to the experience. This we hold to be true however strong the will to achieve may be in even the best artists, and even though we may imagine that to some the value of this assertion of will in their achievement may be greater, in the long run, than any other value the art possesses, greater even than its aesthetic value.

CHAPTER FIVE

IMAGINATION AND GENIUS

IF, THEN, we need not accept as the characteristic mark of art either the pursuit of immortality or the application of social pressure, but may retain our original description of it as an imaginative synthesis of difference into unity, a synthesis distinguished from that of religious devotion by the irrelevance to it of any conviction of external truth—if this is still our definition of the aesthetic, it is time we approached one or two of the most formidable problems it presents. None of these problems is completely soluble at the present time. No theory can yet explain to us successfully what genius is or how it is produced; no theory has given us any practicable formula for determining "greatness" in art, nor shown us in definite terms what elements in an aesthetic experience are contributed by the beholder and what inhere in the stimulating object. Some of these problems we shall return to later. But it is first essential that we attempt to define a little more closely our meaning in the use of certain terms.

The words *imagination* and *imaginative* have appeared already too often without definition. I have said that imagination is the means through which aesthetic synthesis is secured, both in the creator and in the enjoyer. But there is no accepted or standard definition of imagination. The term is, in fact, extremely unfashionable in modern psychology, though it still flourishes almost as freely as ever among literary and art critics. But since the decline of the psychology of the "faculties" and with the rise of repressions, drives, instincts, and conditioning, *imagination* has lost its place. The attention of psychologists has been fixed mainly upon such problems as perception or memory, or else upon motive, particularly unconscious motive. Those few accounts of imagination that have been attempted of late have not succeeded in getting themselves woven into the general fabric of philosophical or psychological thought. And yet the term itself undoubtedly stands for something that has a real part in human life. It may represent a *way of behaving* rather than, as was once supposed, a separate mental faculty; even so, it is still a term with a meaning, however difficult that meaning may be to get at.

No pretense can be made here to solve completely the mysteries of imagination, but I think that the imaginative *process* can be described, at least in part and tentatively. Imagination, then, as I understand it, is not a special or independent faculty: it is a particular way of bringing out into conscious use material from the unconscious or subconscious mind. In using these terms *unconscious* and *subconscious* I do not mean to follow strictly the theory of the psychoanalytic school but only to postulate a human mind of many layers of operation, ranging indefinitely from most to least conscious. How far the degree of consciousness depends upon the phenomenon of attention and how far upon blocking or inhibiting or conflict is irrelevant to our purpose here.

But there are two more or less distinguishable ways in which we bring to conscious use that which had been unconscious. One is primarily logical and analytic; the other is not. It is this other non-logical way that we call imaginative. We seem to have the power of *subjecting this material to our attention*, and yet at the same time of *allowing it to remain free of the mind's rational control*. Why or how this occurs, and why the power to do it varies from time to time and from person to person, we do not know.

Beyond this degree of definition we perhaps cannot go until more is learned about the processes of human thought, conscious or unconscious. Only this should be noticed in regard to the freedom of imagination from rational control, and it is important: that such freedom implies something in the temperament of the individual who possesses it—an absence of fear in respect to certain kinds of inner or mental experience, a willingness to take chances, a certain adventurousness of spirit which makes the possessor willing to give over control, for the moment, to something of which he does not logically see the end. This characteristic of the imaginative person we can perhaps realize empirically by recalling the lack of it in individuals whom we think of as conspicuously unimaginative. They impress us often as being under a compulsion to stick to facts, as though facts should constitute a kind of safety—as though, once you get beyond facts, or become aware of the spaces between them, you have lost control of the outcome, you "never know where you may end". And that, to the unimaginative, is a distressing state of mind.

The material of the imagination, then, we say is what goes on in the unconscious mind. But we should not think of this unconscious material as limited to those drives, repressions, or instincts that psychology has been studying in recent years. In the largest sense, no learning process, no two connected perceptions, are possible without reference to the unconscious area of being. Even the strictest logic, that is, consists not in an unbroken line of knowledge but in a series of jumps, the direction of these jumps being determined more by unconscious than by conscious process.—But we must not here fall into the epistemological bog. The essential point is that wherever we are aware that we are jumping, we are there using imagination. In logic we are not really aware of any hiatus: we recognize it only theoretically; practically, each step seems inevitable, and bound to the preceding one with no unknown area between. But imaginative thought leaps in the dark and knows that it does so; its results come to the light of awareness but its processes do not. All thought, of course, is partly imaginative in its constitution: differences among individuals between the "imaginative" and the "unimaginative" are differences in the degree to which they trust themselves to imagination, and not by any means a difference between the possession or non-possession of a faculty. Not only that. The imaginative individual will often (not always) be found to be more logical than the unimaginative. This is no paradox. For since the criterion is the awareness, not the existence, of the areas between what is felt to be known, the possessor of a keen logical mind should be better equipped for recognizing those areas—providing he is not too timid to do so.

This is imagination in general, and it is the same imagination that plays its part in aesthetic experience. Its apparently special character in relation to beauty is due not to any essential difference in the imaginative process itself, but rather to its purpose, and to the effect of that purpose upon the process. Because the purpose is to achieve an experience of unity in an area where we feel that logical or rational thought is inadequate to achieve it, imagination becomes necessarily the dominant element in aesthetic production.

But where does the "creative imagination" come in? And where the whole difference, so fundamental in modern, if not in primitive cultures, between the power of the artist and that of his audience?—for thus far we have treated the entire subject as if the two were one.

The phenomenon of genius is among the most difficult of all the problems in the psychology of art. And here again, although we cannot hope to work out a wholly adequate theory, it may be worth while to add whatever we can to the accepted picture. One difference, perhaps, can be pointed out between the creator and what we may as well call, lacking a better name, the enjoyer of art. It is not a point of primary importance, for it does not show any difference between the powers of the two but only marks a difference in what the experience feels like to the individuals. And the truth even of this can be checked only by introspective observation. This difference is that in the creative process a man is able to "let go", to let his imagination sail out, conscious of being alone, though with a sort of second self for company. This feeling of being on a lone adventure I think forms a very distinctive part of the characteristic mental state in which all creative work is done. The appreciator, on the other hand, is always aware that he is accompanied in his imaginative venture by another real person not himself. This is part of what we mean by the "self-sufficiency of the artist", and by the much worn and also much questioned statement that he writes or paints "only for himself".[1] He does, indeed, compose with an audience in mind, but that audience is (I believe this will be confirmed by those who know the experience) a sort of self-created Siamese twin, an imaginary audience precisely like himself. Or, to define the experience perhaps more accurately, the twin that he creates for his audience is a sort of ideal self, a self that maintains all his most certain standards. The experience of creating, therefore, is always a somewhat "split" state. But it is not like most pathological states of mind, split either with conflict or to avoid it. There may be conflicting elements present as no doubt there always are in the mind, but the characteristic feeling of this creating imaginative state is of the *likeness* and the *working together* of the two selves, the difference between them being that of an active and a passive part in the events, and not that of, for example, a self that desires experience and a self that fears it.

Extraordinary self-sufficiency characterizes the creating mind while it is creating: no other person is necessary to it. This extreme detachment is undoubtedly one of the reasons for the awe and reverence and also, on the other hand, for the extreme irritation, which have always characterized society's attitude toward the artist. Most of us will recall having been in the company of some person who was busy with imaginative creation at least in a

[1] If this at first appears contradictory to our earlier account of the artist's desire for fame, which naturally involves creating for the public, I think the contradiction will be seen to disappear by virtue of the distinction there made: that the desire for fame accounts only for some of the energy that goes into creation, and not for the kind of activity that takes place.

minor way. And we shall recall, I think, having felt in such a person a below-the-surface detachment from other people that seems even from the outside to differ from the oblivion of a reader buried in a detective story or of a listener engrossed in a symphony.

It may be asked: If imagination implies the giving over of rational control within the mind, are not imagination and madness the same thing? It is true, of course, that genius and madman have from time immemorial been called cousin. But it is necessary to describe a little more closely what is meant by this freedom from control. To begin with, it does not much matter whether we exclude from the province of imagination the delusions of the insane or the irrational misconceptions of the neurotic. We may call them all imagination if we like. Only, the sane imagination works within the framework of what society considers to be known fact, whereas the insane one does not. I am no mental pathologist and cannot attempt an exact definition of the phenomena of imagination that occur in mental illness. But the sane man carries on both rational and irrational processes together. His imagination, his leaps in the dark are fairly well confined to *areas in which both he and society would agree that his rational knowledge is incomplete*. He often trips; that is, he often experiences conflict between his imaginative and his rational processes. But both continue interwoven, and the conflict between them never completely inhibits either process.

The man of genius, however, has a further power, though how he comes by it we do not know. He has a strikingly great power of harmonizing to his own satisfaction and to that of others his rational and his irrational processes. In bringing to the surface of consciousness the content of his unconscious mind, and letting it take him where it will, he somehow has the skill to steer, without interruption to his speed, past all the rocks, so that never a fact pierces his hull. And indeed, more remarkable still, he comes to the end of his ride (and so do all who go with him) in possession of a map of his whole river, rocks as well as current.

Here I confess to having concealed ignorance behind an analogy. And I am in danger of asserting a contradiction of freedom and no-freedom in imagination. What I mean to suggest, however, is a kind of flexibility in the power of genius to put on and take off control in such a way that not only is there, relatively speaking, no conflict between his imagination and the world's knowledge (or what he and the world take to be knowledge) but that very often he seems even to have shed a new light upon, or shown in a new perspective, that very knowledge itself. This flexibility, this power to move freely and quickly back and forth between the logical and the imaginative activity, enables him to assemble harmoniously a more complex set of relations than the ordinary man can assemble.

One other characteristic of genius I think may be described. The man of genius appears, at least from the outside, to experience an extraordinarily wide swing between what he includes within his self and what he does not. We all vary from time to time in the degree of what used to be known as our "subjectivity" and our "objectivity"; that is, in how much of experience or of the external world is felt to be within our own selfhood. The unselfconscious person, for example, objectifies very little of his experience, separates very little from himself in order to look at it as something "else". A person who is "self-conscious", on the other hand, permits as little as possible to remain undifferentiated to his consciousness: he objectifies as much as he can.

The man of genius swings from one extreme to the other. His self, in the first place, seems to occupy tremendous space. What has often been remarked upon as the characteristic egotism of the artist is indeed essential to him. Every man of genius must I think at times appear a monstrous child, complacent and impervious. He has a sure and broad and unconscious conviction of the universal validity of his own experience. Each one of us, of course, is the center of his own universe. But the man of genius is so with a much greater feeling of security; the platform of his egotism is much broader, and he is not always being teased with a feeling of guilt for its being so. He is, in this sense, oblivious of whatever he has not included within his self; and his self cannot be impinged upon from outside. But then he swings away from this feeling. Something—we cannot say what—makes him begin to objectify a part of all that has been himself, and this objectifying movement becomes the immediate source of his creative acivity. In the first stage he was less conscious than most intelligent men; he now becomes far more acutely conscious than the rest of us ever are, of whatever it is that he is objectifying. And in this objectifying process, artistic *form* is born.

If we knew what causes this movement to take place, then indeed we might claim to know something of genius. But even this description of his temperament I think helps us to see why so many contradictory things are said of artists. They are sometimes spoken of as highly conscious individuals, sometimes as absent-minded or oblivious. They are said to be very wise; and, equally, to be very child-like. They are regarded as having un-analytical minds; and yet their mastery of a technique would not be possible without genuine intellectual power. These qualities will no longer seem contradictory, however, if the self in general is looked upon as a process and not a fixed entity; and if then the self of the genius is seen to shift farther in both directions than the selves of the rest of us.

Such suggestions as have been made here about the creative imagination and genius are not put forward as solving any mysteries. By describing genius or any aspect of it, we are in no way accounting for the fact that it occurs in some persons and not in most. Nor are we even able to show whether genius is a mere fortuitous co-incidence of various circumstances of the individual's constitution, inherited or otherwise, with his social con-ditioning and "the spirit of the age"; or whether it is a single "gift". We may have opinions about these things, but we have no good evidence, subjective or otherwise. All that we can hope to do by describing the processes of genius from a new angle is to shuffle the unknown quantities about in our minds a little, or to push our definition from the left- to the right-hand corner—leaving a blank perhaps as large as before. If the dialectical theory is correct, we may hope that when we have finished pushing darkness from one place to another someone else may be able to bring in a little light.

CHAPTER SIX

THE MEDIUM

IF OUR interpretation of the aesthetic motive has any truth or value, we should be able to trace some relations more important than the scattered ones that we have heretofore discussed, between this motive and such qualities as are common to all the arts. If the various activities we call art have been gradually organized by man more or less deliberately to increase the frequency or power of those moments of aesthetic experience which occur, sometimes by chance and often by intention, scattered through all human life—if this is true, then the means by which the aesthetic effect is strengthened through the arts should be to some degree observable.

The two characteristics which appear to be peculiar to all the arts and to the arts alone are the use of conventionally given and definitely limited mediums, and the invariable presence of what we call form. We should see, then, whether these things have anything in particular to do with the imaginative unification of reality.

One of the strangest things that man has done—though we rarely think of it so—in organizing his artistic activity, is to conventionalize it by permitting it to make use only of certain definitely limited materials. Of these there are a great many if we consider the fine arts and all the applied arts; yet their limitation is more remarkable than their range. What I mean is most clearly shown in the "imitative" arts of painting and sculpture. The first is limited to the representation of three-dimensional objects by means of pigments applied to a two-dimensional surface. The other uses a medium of stone or some other relatively hard substance, incapable in itself of movement or change, to represent subjects which, whatever else they may be, are always predominantly soft in texture, and characterized by movement—human beings or animals usually. Whatever may be the significance of this kind of limitation, so easily marked out in the representational arts, it is worth noting that almost the only subjects *not* represented in these materials are subjects which are the same as the medium itself or which closely resemble it. We do not paint a picture the whole subject of which is a picture, or a flat wall surface, or a sheet of paper or canvas—of anything, in fact, that suggests two dimensions rather than three. Nor do we ever find a statue of a stone or of a tree trunk except where these are used as technical aids—as the structural supports for a figure, for example. A stone wall, a tree trunk, a house, a rocky promontory are never a sculptor's central subjects. Yet they are not essentially unsuited to art, for they may be represented by a painter or a poet. It is only that they are too *like* the sculptor's medium to be significantly represented through its means.

It is true that in some recent movements in art we find real or apparent exceptions to this rule. The medium of the painter, for example, has been altered by some artists so as to be very slightly three-dimensional by the use of thick incrustations of paint; and with very recent experimental painters we may find other material as well as another dimension used: a painted coat may have actual brass buttons fastened to the canvas. It is not possible yet to judge the artistic value of the works represented by this last type of painting; and since it cannot —at least at present—be said that any of this is great art, we need not attempt to fit it into any principle. But there are many liberties that even the most modern artist does not take with his medium. He does not, for example, carve a stone statue of a bear and then cover the stone with pieces of bear skin.

This fact has long been recognized in other terms as a basic principle of representative art. To go no farther back than the eighteenth century, Sir Joshua Reynolds, who voiced for the most part the accepted views of his day, called attention to the distinction between imitation and deception. A picture or statue should never deceive us into thinking it is anything *except* a picture or statue. A wax figure of a man dressed and painted to look as real as possible is not a work of art, though—or, more accurately—*because* it may be mistaken for a man upon a casual inspection. But if the central experience of art is what we have described it to be, our reason for rejecting exact imitation is not only what has usually been given by Reynolds or others—our dislike of being actually deceived, or the fact that exact imitation is "merely mechanical" and does not require originality or genius to produce—though these are real enough objections. More fundamental is the requirement that the medium of art must be perceived as being entirely unlike the object represented through it, and this must be so in order to fulfill our demand for "unity in variety". That which is to be brought together to create our illusion of oneness in a work of art must represent *difference* to start with. For the artist in seeking unity is not altogether obeying what the psychologists call a regressive impulse, is not attempting to flee from complex reality to the simple homogeneity of infant life or the more complete homogeneity of the womb. He is taking complex reality and *doing something with it*, though what he does with it is to make it seem like one. But the unity of art could mean nothing to him unless it were a unity made out of different elements. This requirement is buried so deeply in the conventions of the medium in painting and sculpture that we hardly realize its existence, though we obey it almost without exception.

In metaphor, as in all art, the things seen imaginatively to be like, must at the same time be known logically to be unlike. Otherwise the click of surprise-recognition, fiction-truth, incongruity all made congruous and one, is lacking. Art in one sense indeed is metaphor rendered infinitely complex. Both may fail or succeed for the same reasons. A metaphor, for example, may be weak on either one of two counts. The different elements brought together may be already so closely unified in our logical thinking that the imaginative fusion seems a supererogation and therefore dull, trivial, or obvious—for it will be recalled that we do not have an aesthetic feeling, whether from a metaphor or from a larger art work, about that which at the moment we regard as logically known or understood. Hence to a small child the statement that snow is frozen water might well be a beautiful metaphor, a work of art in little. It is not, of course, a genuine metaphor, for it has less to do with comparison than with statement of fact. But to a child, for whom the non-identity of water and snow in terms of sense perception would be the obvious truth, such a statement might well bring out a faintly acknowledged underlying similarity with imaginative force. To a scientific person the statement would very likely appear as an inaccurate statement of fact, as a half truth or a platitude; it would not produce upon him any aesthetic impression because it would be so nearly a logical truth: the chemical likeness between snow and water would be the important and well-known fact to him, and the unknown and unlike features—the great difference that they present to our sense perceptions—he would be likely to ignore.

It seems probable that our establishing such rigidly limited mediums as we have established is due in part to our unconscious recognition of this principle of unlikeness that furnishes the basis of metaphor. By choosing to produce our artistic creations mostly in these set mediums we ensure their at least potentially aesthetic character: there will anyhow, that is, be a fixed something —canvas and paint, let us say—against which almost any subject matter one can think of would be different. Or, as we may express it otherwise, part of the artist's subject is given him in advance by the convention of the medium he uses. The stage is set for him, the aesthetic problem posed automatically by his acceptance of the medium. And painters would always have known, long before the principle had ever been verbalized, that their subject must not be too like their medium.

This principle of essential unlikeness is recognized in various other ways. The commonly uttered objection to mere photographic painting is one expression of it. What we commonly give now, in contrast to Sir Joshua's day, as our objection to this literal kind of representation is that such a painting shows no "personality". This no doubt has something to do with it, but it is not our main objection. After all, if we like nature as well as we say we do, we might expect to be pleased with the most exact reproduction possible of natural objects. And we sometimes are. But the point is that in *art* we are looking for something else; we desire not merely to be reminded of our love for nature. We are seeking imaginative unification; and this is not to be achieved by literal imitation, because imitation will arouse our logical power of comparison to test its accuracy, rather than our imaginative power. This explains, for example, the modern preference for unpainted statuary: a statue painted to look "too much" like the real thing offends our taste. Anything, in fact, which can be described as literal representation is looked upon with suspicion from the artistic standpoint. This is true in spite of the many times that we find ourselves or others admiring an object for the exactness with which it imitates something else. Admiration is not the same as an aesthetic response, but we sometimes confuse the two concepts in practice because we often feel admiration for the skill of the artist as well as aesthetic pleasure in his production. And so we sometimes in thought mistake, for example, an admiration for the skill and the patience of a man who has made a piece of metal reproduce the exact grain and color of wood, for an aesthetic enjoyment of his production. More often, we make the same mistake in admiring a painting which exhibits such skill in the imitation of fabric or texture that "you almost think you could feel the velvet" or "you almost smell the fruit".

Though we sometimes misinterpret our feeling in such ways as these, persons who have thought about art make a clear distinction between "imitation" in unlike terms which is genuinely aesthetic, and imitation by reproduction, which is not. Only, even for thoughtful persons as for artists themselves the line between one and the other may sometimes become blurred. Extreme cases are clear, but many borderline ones are not. Artists, for instance, have often tried to paint a glorious sunset, though many would say at once that this cannot be done. Aesthetically, the attempts have almost if not quite invariably failed. And the reason seems to be, not that the sunset is too beautiful to be painted, but rather that it can be too nearly reproduced in paint. Not quite, of course. The painter's colors have not all the glow and brilliance of the sky, nor so many infinitely fine gradations of color, nor such apparent softness of texture. But one essential difference is not sufficiently acute. For we do not perceive distance accurately in the sky. And therefore, though there may be clouds behind clouds, and we may *know* that there are vast distances in what we see, and our imagination of the vast distances may give us great pleasure, yet actually the sky looks to us rather like a flat or domed surface with perspective *suggested* rather than *visible*. The physical reason for this can be easily explained. As proof of its truth we may recall the frequent discussion about how large the moon looks—the varying answers to which depend not upon our eyesight or accuracy or judgment, but upon the mental perspective that we set up. In other words, the sky already *looks* more like a painting than do most other things in nature. And therefore when it is represented as the chief part of a painting we are dissatisfied with the result. The artist has produced a sunset that is not as unlike a real one—as it ought to be. It seems therefore like an inferior copy of the original and no more.

Another somewhat special case of the same problem was observed by that astute critic, Charles Lamb. In an essay on the art of acting he makes clear the difference between the effect secured by the actor who acts and the actor who is natural. One man may be successful in a given part because the character in the play is like himself and he therefore fits the part naturally. Now, though he may apparently succeed, his acting does not satisfy us aesthetically to any such degree as does that of the truly great actor, who interprets a part through an imaginative understanding of the character he represents and an aesthetic appreciation of the effect of the whole play. Nearly always the beholder, at least if he knows the play well, is aware which kind of performance the actor is giving even in seeing him perform for the first time. This aesthetic superiority of the actor who acts over the actor who is himself is again partly a matter of the necessity for an unlike medium.

The truth of this distinction is most noticeable in comedy, where character types are as a rule more specifically laid out. Mr. Charles Chaplin, for example, would not please us as he does if we were not aware—and we are inevitably aware, even if we know nothing from outside sources about him as a person—that he is *not* the character he represents. By his very acting we know him to be something different from the sweet, foolish person that he represents: we are aware that he is interpreting life through the unifying form of his stage presence. He can personify thus all sorts of meanings. He presents, for instance, in a form which we take in as a felt truth, the

notion that for man to assume self-responsibility of action is at the same time ridiculous and inevitable. That is
only one of the generalizations made concrete in the
attitude of the little shuffling figure, but it pervades the
whole. The character Charlie is always ridiculously inadequate (except sometimes in a conventionally happy
ending) and always gravely responsible; even his clothes
symbolize this: the suit too large, the hat too important,
the shoes too heavy to lift. Through these Charlie sig-
nifies what life demands of him, his mature and grave
responsibilities. And lost inside these symbols of responsibility is the small uncomprehending child-man, doing
his best to fill them out and always through his failure
making the incongruity more sharply ridiculous. But the
character would not have the power of an aesthetic
symbol if Chaplin the actor were felt to be merely that
foolish little person. We assimilate, through all his convincing presentation of the character, his own comment
as well—or rather his shaping mind unifying his character with his own comment.

Our preference for this kind of acting has, to be sure,
other causes—at least two in addition to our demand for
unlikeness between medium and subject. The first is another aesthetic consideration: that the "natural" actor
breaks up the unity of the play. If he is simply being
himself, his every gesture, tone, and movement are not
being subjected to the purposes of the whole. And since
no play presents characters in their natural totality, but
only in their relations to other parts of the dramatic
whole, an actor cannot achieve the greatest aesthetic
effect without being an interpreter.

A second consideration that enters here is a non-
aesthetic but important one. Sir Joshua Reynolds spoke

—as almost any artist will—with scorn of mere "mechanical" copyists. Humanity respects the person who can without destruction to society assert his will independently. In art he can scarcely do it without great intelligence, great skill, and great power to experience life in one way or another: and these are also qualities that humanity admires. Hence we tend to admire the artist or actor in his own person and because of his own powers, as well as to enjoy his creations. Some actors who are not really creative actors but who have likeable personalities which they present quite naturally on the stage we may enjoy going to see, because we like to know pleasant, or funny, people. But we like even better to make the more difficult acquaintance of the true actor who presents something else than himself and who therefore has to be seen more often to be known as himself. Neither of these pleasures is strictly speaking aesthetic, but both are likely to play a considerable part in all aesthetic activity. Indeed, this desire to make the acquaintance of the person behind the work of art is one of the most characteristic differences between the aesthetic activity of modern times and that of ancient, still more of primitive ages. But it is a change in other values of the activity surrounding aesthetic experience, and not, as many historical students of art have indicated, a change in that experience itself.

The ways, then, in which we perceive the need for unlikeness between medium and subject may range from the most obvious—the quite universal recognition that visiting a waxwork museum is not an aesthetic adventure —to a much more subtle recognition of differences required in which neither artist nor critic nor any of us is infallible. About the art of acting, it is still almost universally believed that one should be the part entirely, though this belief may represent only an incomplete analysis of the playgoer's experience and not an actual preference for the most nearly exact identity of person and part. And there are perhaps many other failures in art which we have recognized but not analyzed, that might be traced to an unobserved resemblance between medium and subject, such as that suggested in the painting of sunsets.

The degree or the kind of unlikeness between medium and subject required by any art varies somewhat from age to age and from individual to individual. Like every other generalization about art, we can formulate it, but we cannot mark off with exactness the boundaries of its application. Sculpture has, for example, in certain periods been painted over, at times probably in a somewhat realistic manner. And there are unquestionably people who have found aesthetic satisfaction in paintings of a sunset—as well as in tinted photographs of a moonlit sky. In the case of ancient sculpture, we are too far from the civilization to which it belonged to be able to guess what likeness or unlikeness they were aware of. With our individual contemporaries, however, who enjoy the painted sunsets or moonrise, it will probably be found rather like our case of the metaphor: if the beholders have had little experience of art there will be for them perhaps enough of unlikeness in the medium and in the circumstances, because of the knowledge forced upon them by their surroundings if by nothing else that they are looking at a picture—this will be enough to mark off the medium from the thing represented. The vivid consciousness, that is, that they are looking at "a mere picture", which yet resembles a sunset or moonrise, gives them a keener awareness of difference between medium and subject than occurs with the person to whom art is more familiar or more important, who therefore accepts without noticing it this elementary difference and requires for his aesthetic satisfaction some additional differences. So that, as an art grows older and gathers thicker layers of convention, more complex likeness-difference relationships must be added as the older customary ones cease to be noticed.

In acknowledging the artist's need to keep his medium recognizably distinct from his subject matter, we have, however, to note that there must also be a limit to the degree of this difference. Medium and content must be different, indeed; but they must obviously be at least simultaneously conceivable. The idea of a picture painted to represent a sound, for example, to most people is not even an idea: it has no meaning at all. Although, since the rise of the Symbolist movement in France, there have been recurrent efforts to break through each artistic medium and to use one in terms of another, no change of this kind has come to be established as a new convention, and the arts are still on the whole distinct in this respect. This truth, that *some* degree of likeness between medium and subject is essential, has been more elaborately explored by writers on aesthetics than has the opposite one. Especially since the publication of Lessing's *Laocoon*, much thought has been given to the limitation of subject matter implied in spatial mediums as compared with temporal ones. This point does not appear to demand further exploration at the present time, but a third point does. That is the function of the artistic medium in contributing to the effect of unity. The artist does not work through all the materials of life, altering and combining all sorts of objects and experience into a unified whole. As far as his subject matter goes, he does this with almost complete freedom. But for the expression of it, he projects all the variety of his subject upon a medium which has an artificially created singleness.

In life, for instance, a dinner party might be almost a work of art—might certainly produce an aesthetic impression upon someone present. But it is not projected, as art is, upon a single medium. The relations between the chosen guests, the seating arrangement, the room, the appointments, the service, the food—all these may happen to be elements that amalgamate into an aesthetic whole. But no one of these elements is the fixed and unifying medium upon which the rest are projected. The hostess may have the capacity of an artist in creating this kind of unity, but her medium has neither the permanence nor the singleness nor the likeness-indifference power of art. The aesthetic effect cannot be communicated or re-experienced (except perhaps less vividly in memory) because there is no permanent medium; and the elements are not as likely to become fused into one whole because there is no single medium, no prevailingly similar material by means of which (partly) difference is absorbed. It might be said that the method of art creates unity by two distinct stages: that it reduces the multiple to the dual, subject and medium, and then unifies these two by means of form.

The complete translation of subject into medium is one of the greatest means we have of securing an aesthetic effect. Most critics, in fact, would consider this power of translation a sine qua non for a great artist. Yet not every artist, not even every famous one, possesses this power in an eminent degree. How it comes to him we are at present unable to say, but it is more than a mere matter of mechanical skill or practice, and is in part at least a peculiar way of using the imagination. We are familiar with such expressions from critics as that a man "has a feeling for his medium" or that he lacks it, and that another "thinks" in paint or in marble.

Perhaps the most illuminating general exposition in recent years of the artist's use of medium occurs in S. Alexander's *Beauty and Other Forms of Value*. Professor Alexander, approaching his subject at an angle different from ours, analyzes a truth about the artist's relation to his medium with remarkable insight. The artist, he says, does not actually know what his own conception is with any precision until he has actually embodied it in the medium. It is not true, he contends—though the belief is common—that a great artist first may have a complete and perfect vision of his finished whole, and then proceed to work until his final product matches his original vision. Rather the process is one of finding out what he means, or creating his own vision as he goes, this vision being by no means separate from the medium and, as it were, plastered upon it, but only developed *through* it in the actual execution, whether in pigment, marble, words, or anything else. This I believe is a profound and too little recognized truth. The great artist undoubtedly has some vision, more or less definite, of what he intends to produce, but his work of creation is actually a clarifying and an exploring of that intention for himself in terms of his medium.

Artists vary greatly in the degree of difficulty which they experience in using their medium; but even the most facile probably regard it often as something to be overcome. One modern poet, who is not verbally facile, describes the labor of composition as an effort to compel friendliness out of hostility, to "bring the medium over on your side so that it works with and not against you." Whether it is a case of easy mastery or of difficult conquest—and it may be either—the great artist makes the medium part of the whole. And in so doing he forges for himself what we call his style.

This final fusion, not only of all the meanings of a work of art with each other, but of meanings with medium as well—so that the medium becomes in fact part of the total meaning—this fusion, though it is essential for the complete achievement of the greatest art, is not, as we have already said, by any means universal even among highly respected artists. Sometimes it is achieved only in spots or passages here and there. Sometimes an artist just misses real greatness because he never or rarely succeeds in making his medium contribute to his unity. This whole point is so important—to see what can and what cannot be achieved in art when the imaginative assimilation of the medium is incomplete—that it is worth while trying to illustrate it by reference to a fairly well-known modern instance.

Thomas Hardy has been pretty widely acclaimed as a great artist in both poetry and the novel. Yet the best critics have often found fault with his style, and have complained that he "had no feeling for words." George Moore, who should know style—for he himself began as a writer without one, without any true relation to his medium, and gradually worked through to a good one—made a famous destructive analysis of a patch of prose from *Far From the Madding Crowd*, in which he showed, among other things, how little relation existed between Hardy's obvious intention and the words he used. Almost anywhere in Hardy's writing the same kind of analysis might be made. He could not use phrases or words with all the accrued meanings and half-meanings, the associations, the groupings that have come traditionally to have value, in such a way as to give them fresh power to convey his own individual meanings as well. And so most of Hardy's writing in either poetry or prose gives the effect of leaving the medium out. The words trail behind; there is a banality in them as if the artist's mind is not there, animating them into life. The sentences assemble one after another, but emptily: nobody is at home. Or the style is like an amateur actor who keeps falling in and out of his part. Hardy's words are used now with meaning and now merely to fill out a sentence, or are allowed to go idly speaking on after his mind has left them. The words serve only to give us a general account of the meaning, and do not seem to create it. The fault is not in his vision of what he wants to do, nor in his characters, nor in the unifying power of his mind in terms of subject matter or philosophy; but rather in his lack of an intimate feeling for the validity of words.

For this reason, the effect he produces upon readers is not altogether an aesthetic one. Readers like and admire one of his novels because of the view presented of a particular kind of English life, or because they have strong sympathy with Hardy's philosophy, his unified view of the world, or because they share his attachment to nature, or because they admire his courage in flouting Victorian convention, or because they are fascinated by his odd personal mixture of pessimism and gusto, which seems to show us by example that one can think ill of the universe and yet be personally not un-happy—or for all these and many other reasons. They value in Hardy, that is, many of the qualities one would value in an exceptionally interesting acquaintance in real life. But only occasionally is the experience of read-ing Hardy aesthetic.

In *The Return of the Native*, perhaps, the imagina-tive unification of all the elements except style is so powerful that in retrospect, if not during the actual reading of the book, an aesthetic whole is felt. The heath so dominates human life there, and certain of the heath scenes are described with such an almost cosmic wildness, that we feel as if the whole book were pervaded by earth and gloomy sky, "Chaos and Old Night", and Fate. An artist does sometimes achieve an aesthetic effect of the whole like this even in a medium which he cannot make to help him. His lack of relish for his medium then impairs the effect of all the indi-vidual parts without quite destroying the retrospectively felt power of the whole. A reader will at once see in the opening chapter of *The Return of the Native* the fine-ness of Hardy's conception, the dramatic power of his use of human figure and background—figure and back-ground being reversed in importance. The heath is pre-sented in general, at noon, then in the hour before dark, with all the cosmic overtones of the suggestions of space, day and night, wind and cloud passing by on their great journeys. And then at the end of the chapter, as if seen from a great imaginary height, the figure of a man travels slowly across the face of the heath—only a figure, no more. This is very fine. Hardy's sense of the propor-tion and relation between human beings and nature or fate is symbolized in this scene, which stands almost as

a parable for the meaning of the whole book. Throughout the novel the various presentations of the heath
have great unity: the heath with fires at night, alive with
small figures of people; or solitary with the half silence,
the "papery rustling" of withered heath bells; or black
like a painting by Rembrandt with a center of light
from a single lantern, shining dimly upon faces, hands,
dice, and the white noses of curious wild ponies who
edge near and flee at a sudden movement. These scenes
are vividly conceived and related with a fine dramatic
sense to the human lives over which they preside. And
they give to the reader's memory the tone of the whole
book. But a reader sensitive to the use of language finds
the actual writing of each one of these scenes full of
waste words, weak repetition, aimless and ineffectual
sentences, even bits of descriptive material or allusions
that lack accuracy or pertinence of mood. The idea in
the mind was fine—and it was an aesthetic one—but it
does not become completely embodied in words so that
words and meaning are all one. This is why the book in
retrospect seems better aesthetically than it does while
it is being read, just as thinking of each of the fine heath
scenes gives greater aesthetic pleasure than does the reading of them.

In other novels of Hardy there are finely conceived
scenes—an early morning dairy scene in *Tess* stands out
among them—but in none of these novels is there such
an aesthetic organization or form that an aesthetically
satisfactory whole is possible without a less refractory
or unrealized style. In prose, only when he uses dialect
does Hardy seem to establish any significant relation to
his medium.

Verse, by the mere exigencies of its form, forces a

writer to come to terms a little more closely with his medium. And although Hardy's poetry shows a great deal of the same character as his prose, the same looseness, the same filling out of sentence or line—in fact, all the same characteristics of what is generally called poor workmanship as well as a lack of that more subtle *complete* infusion of words with meaning—in spite of these failings, his verse shows in some places a kind of determined, forcible use of language, as if, not having been able to win over his medium to friendly aid, he were hammering it out, forging it into a somewhat usable tool. His poetry is therefore full of abrupt, unidiomatic sequences of words, as if he had rifled the dictionary, torn words from their usual contexts, and by pure force of will set them down side by side and bullied them into a kind of wary friendliness. Wherever he does this he achieves a unity that in some degree includes his medium, though it is an odd one. But this does not occur as often as Hardy's enthusiastic admirers suppose, and it rarely carries through a whole poem. Where he does not use language in this way he does not achieve great or even good poetry. The *idea* of almost any of his poems is susceptible of poetic treatment, but not often are his vision of unity and his imagination intense enough to make him embody the idea completely in a concrete form that includes instead of disregards the words; only rarely, therefore, does his poetry come to life in any but intellectual terms. A competent writer, by retelling quite briefly Hardy's plan and intention in *The Return of the Native*, by describing briefly the effect of the heath in some of its moods, borrowing a few of the best-chosen epithets as he goes, can create as strong an aesthetic impression upon his reader as the whole of

Hardy's novel itself does.[1] This is a consequence of the lack of fusion between Hardy's subject and his medium: that his own words are not necessary to the production of whatever aesthetic effect he does produce. And Hardy will cease to be read if ever another writer makes approximately the same synthesis in such a way as to include the language within that synthesis.

This digression upon Hardy is not altogether, I hope, a digression. It is sometimes difficult to keep clear the difference between medium and form, and Hardy provides one of the most precise illustrations of this difference, for he is conspicuously weak in relation to his medium, and not so at all in respect to form. It is therefore relatively easy to view one without the other in his work.

---

[1] Except possibly for the advantage given by mere duration. The actual length of time required to read the novel gives it some advantage, for depth of impression, over a good summary. But it is the only advantage.

CHAPTER SEVEN

FORM

To SOME extent medium and form have the same function. The medium contributes to the unity of the whole, as we have seen, through its uniformity or its relatively unchanging character; form has no other end than the achievement of this unity.

Our discussion of form, however, involves a revision of much else that has been said. Hitherto we have been treating certain pairs of opposites as if their character as logical opposites were their total real character. The oppositions of the one and the many, the self and the world-without, of homogeneous and heterogeneous, content and form—these are logical distinctions whose opposition does indeed have a real meaning in experience. But nothing in life is as simple or clear-cut as this, and already we have seen the strict opposition of one of these pairs, *self* and *world-without*, break down in the discussion of genius. Our use of these as if they were the simple reality is, in fact, a concession to human preference in thought. We have never approached a development in thinking power by which we might treat all reality as relative instead of absolute. Though the absolute is surely a bird whose tail we shall never salt, no one knows whether we shall ever stop pursuing it. We never have. Perhaps the doctrines of Darwin and Einstein are an indication that we are beginning to transcend this need for an absolute; on the other hand, there is some evidence that we may be using scientific relativity only to build up a new kind of absolute, new springes to catch the same woodcocks.

When we speak of the aesthetic as creating an imaginative unity between the self and the world-without, then, we are assuming a clearer opposition than we can justify. Roughly, self and non-self are mutually exclusive and are easily identified. But even the unphilosophical man may ask himself whether food in the stomach is part of his self—or a tear in the eye. Whether the self is conceived as bounded by a physiological or a psychic line, and where its boundaries in time are to be drawn are nice questions and not merely speculative ones. Similarly, when we define form in art as our means of controlling external reality for the purpose of imaginative unification—of making it one with ourself—we believe that we are stating a truth, but we hasten to qualify it. For many elements of what we call form inhere in or are suggested so strongly by even our most literal view of external reality, as not to seem altogether imposed by our minds. Again, form itself, regarded from one standpoint, actually becomes a part of the content. This is most obvious in pure design. Take, for example, a two-dimensional design whose constituent parts are circles; these are thought of as pure form when taken alone, but they appear here as the *content* of the larger design. Not only this. For although we talk of multiplicity as found in the world-without, and unity in the self, we are not being accurate. The self is aware of almost as much that is not unified *within* as *without*. In fact, multiplicity in the external world would very likely not disturb us at all if it were not reflected by multiplicity, and hence conflict, within.

These, however, are psychological and philosophical problems, universal and all-important, but neither possible nor necessary to analyze here. Only it should be noted that feeling, which is thought of primarily as *content* in art (*vide* the common view that art is the expression of emotion), often has the unifying function of form. This we may recognize by recalling the familiar judgment that a work lacks or conspicuously possesses "unity of mood". So, though form and content are truly seen as opposites according to logical analysis, what this opposition-concept gives us is a simple abstraction from the real truth. It is therefore only one way of thinking about the subject. Another way is quite as important. This is to consider content and form in art as no more separable than matter and organization in the human body. Matter and organization, many modern philosophers would agree, are different ways of thinking about the living human body, rather than separable aspects of it; their separableness, that is, inheres in these terms as concepts and not in them as objectively real. This is approximately the notion of artistic form that Coleridge tried to establish in literary criticism when he described organic form as the essential for art as against "mechanical" form.

Such a concept of form is not at all new, and it is in fact rather widely accepted in modern aesthetic theory. There are still, it is true, schools of thought in which the importance of form is ignored, in which the essence of art is considered to be its content and its persuasiveness over the feelings by means of a certain (usually unanalyzed) expressive power on the part of the artist, or in which the artist's power is believed to rest in a superior insight into important truths—that is, in his content and not in his form. The writers of these schools of thought have not in general analyzed their idea of form, and conceive it therefore in somewhat superficial terms as making the pattern pretty or producing harmonious color schemes, or giving us the pleasant repetition of refrain in music or verse. But why is the pattern pretty? we must in the end ask. And why are colors harmonious, and repetitions of audible or visible pattern pleasant? It does not quite satisfy us to say that repetition makes things easier to understand or remember. For the human mind can in some degree understand and remember very complex things.

Even such an authority on aesthetics as Bosanquet falls into the habit of referring to form as "mere form", and of supposing that he has disposed of an uncongenial theory when he has complained that it renders art "purely formal"—as if that necessarily means reducing it to triviality. But form is, after all, the residue, many times sifted, of all our power of abstraction from the concrete, re-imposed again on new material in new ways. In a sense, form is the essence of meaning. It is therefore a power over experience and thus can never be conceived of as "mere" form.[1]

If we look upon the aesthetic as the imaginative unification of reality, we at once see almost innumerable ways in which this unification can be achieved; and

---

[1] It is, of course, common to use *form* as synonymous with *pattern*. But to do so is confusing in aesthetic theory. Pattern has its own name. And if *form* is used mainly for this, then all the most important aspects of what we know as form (for pattern is only the most mechanical and trivial of all its manifestations) are left unnamed or unnoticed.

form, which perhaps might be found to include all these means, is seen as the fundamental requirement of art. We are in no better position than Plato—or than Hogarth or Reynolds—to decide whether the most perfect beauty of form is to be found in the circle, the ellipse, the right triangle, or the golden-section rectangle. In fact, this question no longer has meaning for us if the logical opposition and the mutual exclusiveness of *form* and *content* cease to be maintained. Our concept of form must indeed open out so as to include vast areas of experience. And we can trace this form in experience from the simplest suggestion of unity to the most complex sets of interrelations which we can imagine being analyzed into further and further intricacies until, of what looked at first to be substance controlled by form, nothing will be left except form; or, as we described it earlier, the subject becomes all form and no subject remains. The case is comparable to what some physicists did with the old dualism of "matter" and "motion" by analyzing it eventually down into pure "motion" or its modern equivalent. Not that this resolution in either criticism or science has ever been complete; only, this became its goal, whether attainable or not. However, in the case of art it is just as true to say that what began as form and medium have actually become content, since the value of the whole resides in the symbolic unification of all the elements concerned, these included.

Form in art has two aspects, each of which is easily distinguishable in general, though in specific application they melt imperceptibly into each other. These are the *inherited* aspects of form, traditions built up by past artists; and the *original* form, that which is worked out by each artist for the needs of his particular problem.

The distinction between these two elements of form partially, though not wholly, corresponds once more to the Coleridgean distinction between "mechanic" and "organic" form. Only, both elements are present in all first-rate artistic production. There is no need to elaborate this point; it is obvious. Forms that have been named—sonata-form, sonnet, epic—are instances in which the tradition has become so crystallized that they seem almost more like mediums than like forms. In more detailed ways too, of course, the artist inherits his form. The intricate forms within the heroic couplet as developed by Pope have been inherited and used by others; the whole modern contrapuntal "style" in orchestral music, varying as it does with each individual user, nevertheless contains a residue that is common property. These are but single illustrations drawn from the huge bodies of crystallized tradition within which every artist works. Such conventional aspects of form have evolved no doubt partly in the interest of making aesthetic experience more certainly and more exactly sharable. Content fitted into familiar grooves we at once feel more at home with than if we meet it in unfamiliar surroundings. And often within a highly conventional form this advantage of familiarity makes possible the expression of more complex elements than could be completely unified without it.

But a highly conventional form—in fact any convention—has another value. It gives great satisfaction to the artist (and vicariously also to his audience) from pride in being able to assert his individuality within the limits set up by the group. As a form grows more and more rigid through convention, this satisfaction may even increase: the artist is confined within narrower and narrower limits imposed from without, and still, supposing him to be a great artist, his own individual will has power of assertion. He says what he himself alone wills to say. This is one of the great values in what we often speak of a little contemptuously as conventional forms and is, of course, one of the characteristic values of all so-called "classical" art. But whether the inherited form is rigid or flexible, complex or simple, because of its mere presence every work of art has something of this underlying meaning that non-artistic aesthetic experience does not have. A poem or a painting is by its mere existence an assertion of "free-will", for through the symbol furnished by the reconciliation of the individual and the conventional elements of its form, it asserts that freedom is possible. It does not address the assertion to the intellect, which would be sceptical as it always has been. Nor does it address an appeal to our faith to believe the assertion literally. What it does is to make the *idea* of free-will vividly conceivable, or make the idea powerfully present to the mind (even though not formulated intellectually)—so present, indeed, and therefore so subjectively true, so realized or so felt—that the factual truth of it does not for the moment matter at all. As soon as belief in the factual truth comes to be not only present, but the center of importance in the mind, the experience ceases to be aesthetic and becomes religious.

This symbol, to take a simple form for illustration, is perhaps a literary critic's chief meaning when he speaks of the poet's mastery of the sonnet form. It is a familiar saying that "nothing is easier to write than a poor sonnet". By this we mean presumably that the inferior writer in conforming to the general will (the conven-

tional form) loses his power to assert his individual will
and therefore fails to provide that underlying symbolic
meaning that we demand of all great art. The genuine
poet, on the other hand, perhaps finds an idea in his
mind or a phrase or two that begins to run somewhat in
sonnet form as it takes shape. But the poet's idea, and
his will, in all sorts of ways as the poem develops will
run counter to the convention of the sonnet: the word
desired at the end of the line does not rhyme, or something insists on being expressed in a way that breaks the
meter or the line formation. Then at last these differences are ironed out. Sometimes gradually and sometimes suddenly, the idea *becomes* the form. It is as if the
poet instead of fighting the general will had suddenly
turned and accepted it, not passively, but with complete
positive coincidence between his individual will and the
general will as laid down by tradition in the formula.
Sometimes, that is, it may seem as if the poet turned
over and joined society, sometimes as if he won the
social will over to reinforce the assertion of his individual will, and sometimes as if the two, because of the
magnitude or universality of the poet's temper, simply
coincided without effort, as part of the nature of things.

But by whichever way the process occurs, in the result
there will be the poet's content, the given form, and
besides these the many other almost invisible formal
elements through which the poet has made form and
content one. The scarcely discernible balance of inflec-
tions, cadences, pauses; the balance between minute var-
iations of tempo; and all the "patterning" elements
which at their best show forth new facets of the old form,
illuminate it, or reinforce its shape by the subtle corre-
spondence between the given form and the new indi-

vidual formal elements woven into it so that "the sonnet becomes a different thing in this poet's hands", and yet remains a true sonnet; the precise choice of words to bring out formal relations between meanings as well as between sounds—all this the poet does, not through step-wise logic, but through what we must still call by its somewhat question-begging name, *genius*. This is the way he creates his symbol of free-will—whether ultimately real or ultimately illusory we shall not say here, since the choice depends upon one's individual philosophy.

This is one way, at any rate, in which through form the poet's own will and the world's will are united. We may, it is true, be reading into this aspect of the creative process a concept that belongs to the social philosopher. To the poet's feeling or the reader's, the given form of the sonnet may represent not the social will but simply external reality in general. The form may seem so fixed, so given, and so dehumanized by time and use that it is felt to be more related to things than to people. But whether this is so or not, the symbolic meaning of freedom of the will is still there, and it matters little whether this freedom is felt as being achieved in spite of, and at the same time by means of, society, or in spite of "matter".

What we have come to call a man's *style* is merely the individual habitual ways that he develops of achieving this synthesis in relation to the traditionally given elements, the inherited form and medium (not the content). But each great artist's style works in its turn some change upon the tradition of form and medium to be inherited by his successors. Something of what Titian, what Rembrandt, what Cézanne developed in technique or style, as their own personal relation to their medium and their own individual way of relating their content to the traditional form, becomes for today's artist a part of his inherited medium and form itself, just as he also may do something to change it. But these changes, these techniques, if examined closely, prove to be not separable from the content or meaning of the art work, for if they are good ones—that is, if they actually form part of the aesthetic synthesis—they have been developed or invented as an essential means of relating to his medium, as we have said, the artist's own special imaginative view of reality. Thus, for example, to adopt in any degree an infinitely painstaking Dutch painter's *style* in painting a quiet interior, is to experience also in some degree that painter's philosophy or feeling about quiet rooms. And to adopt anything of the Impressionists' style or technique in painting light, is also to adopt something of their philosophy, or of the *feeling* about light which was their subject as much as it was their technique.

It is probable that our breaking down of the distinction between form and content, and our treatment of form and style at one moment as a means to an end and at another moment as an integral part of the end itself, will appear either as logical ineptitude or as an arbitrary attempt to reach a somewhat mystical conclusion. I hope that it is neither. But at the risk of making the impression worse, I should like to attempt to show in some one specific case how far the interrelation of form and content can be traced, show what can be found technically, and why—in a single poem; show, in fact, how the form *drives in* the meaning and then jumps in after, and show how the two appear to become fused in one symbol. To do this I shall take a short poem of A. E. Housman. Anyone who is afraid of having one of the most perfect of modern lyrics spoiled by analysis had better, as Chaucer warns the timid, "turne over the leef and chese another tale". In this kind of attempt, crudeness is inevitable and complete analysis is impossible. Probably only a minute portion of what the poet's imagination has materialized can be described even by himself. For if we knew enough of the elements involved to be able to express them analytically, we should neither need nor desire the aesthetic expression of them. So long, that is, as we *believe* that we understand something, we do not also *deliberately imagine* ourselves understanding it. We cannot forget that the province of the aesthetic is the unknown or, more exactly, the felt-to-be-unknown.

The particular poem has been chosen for several other reasons besides its excellence. In the first place, it is a poem that I had long known and felt to be beautiful without having made any attempt to learn why it was so. Only when I found myself wondering how a poem that appeared so slight in both form and content could convey, in fact transfer, depths of tragic intensity—only then did I become at all aware of its structural character. Analysis was made later and without intention, merely from knowing the poem well and finding this or that formal element suddenly present in my mind. The analysis, therefore, although it may not be true or correct, at any rate is not one made up for a theory and does not grow out of a hunt for vowel correspondences or alliterative patterns, a chase which is sometimes pursued with such determination that patterns will be found or invented, even though the passage contains no more of them than a paragraph of newspaper prose. The formal elements that will be mentioned here are all ones which became apparent without being looked for, and represent, not what *can* be found, but what actually does become noticeable, for one reader at least.

The poem is the first one of Housman's volume *Last Poems*. In it he is saying that he will write no more, is perhaps hinting too that life as well as work is nearly over. The poem appears immediately after the preface in which Housman explained the publication of such a small volume by the fact of his age and the probability that he would write little more. But in the poem he says none of this directly.

> We'll to the woods no more,
> The laurels all are cut,
> The bowers are bare of bay
> That once the Muses wore;
> The year draws in the day
> And soon will evening shut:
> The laurels all are cut,
> We'll to the woods no more.
> Oh we'll no more, no more
> To the leafy woods away,
> To the high wild woods of laurel
> And the bowers of bay no more.

Not only does the poem seem slight on the surface; it seems, if examined apart from the impression it makes, over-conventional in imagery. Have we not had enough by this time of Muses and laurels and bowers of bay? Scarcely a word or image is used that is not pretty well hackneyed and—to the average modern mind—even unsuggestive. And yet the whole is powerful in effect.[1] How does it rise to such a climax, looking as it does simple and quiet as well as conventional? The general meaning of the poem, of course, is not a trivial one; and there would naturally be a certain pathos in seeing the poet as an old man consciously announcing the end of his work. But the effect of the poem is not one of pathos but of tragic dignity. The dignity is achieved partly through the fact that the literal meaning is not once stated but is only implied. The classical use of laurel and bay convey the *fact*: the tragic *importance* of the fact is brought home by means of the kind and extent of repetition.

The factual meaning of the poem is contained in the symbol of its first two lines:

> "We'll to the woods no more,
> The laurels all are cut."

It is like the ideal allegory (which never was written): the symbol absolutely different from the thing symbolized, and yet possessing a hidden affinity with it which is forced upon our attention by the poet's treatment; that is, by his general form, his musical pattern, the inevitable connotations of his words. In common allegory the two layers of meaning are brought together by simple and usually intellectual or arbitrary devices: the castle is named Pride or the giant Sansfoy—which is perhaps why we call Spenser great "in spite of his allegory". In this poem of Housman the two meanings re-

---

[1] For its powerful effect I am not depending upon my own taste only, but upon that of a number of other persons. Besides, it is echoed every now and then by other writers, the most recent echoes that I have noticed being in Thomas Wolfe and W. H. Auden. Nevertheless, those who read very quickly often fail to notice the poem at all.

main separate in the sense that one is spoken and the other unspoken throughout, and yet they are united in the imagination without any aid except what lies in the essence of the symbol itself. The form—even apart from a reference to fame in *laurel* and *bay*—makes us feel that two things are meant where one is said. The opening lines might indeed have been expanded into a pleasant descriptive piece about autumn. Instead, the poet repeats and repeats, narrowing and concentrating his imagery, adding new detail sparingly and only to heighten the impression of the old; so that his form is rather *infolding*, with the repetitiousness of a tragic situation which cannot be escaped and must be dwelt upon, rather than an *outfolding* form, full of change with new imagery in every line, which a different mood would have dictated.[1]

But the poem does not remain static; it grows to a climax in the line before the last, "To the high wild woods of laurel", and particularly in the words "high wild". *Wild* is the only unquiet word in the poem. Though so common a word as to be scarcely noticeable, its force here is almost like a cry in the dark, partly because its choice is felt to be dictated not by the surface meaning but by the underlying meaning: only some such deeper intention would permit the poet to attach the word *wild* to his conventional little bowers of bay. But the force of the word is increased tenfold by means of sound. The identical long vowel in *high*, before it, strengthens the effect: each of the two words, in fact, intensifies the other because, hearing the same dominant sound in both, we grasp them in the same imaginative

[1] A perfect illustration of such a contrasting mood and form would be Herrick's poem "Corinna's Going A-Maying".

unit—the high is made wild and the wild high. But the tension of the moment is partly due also to the fact that no other long-i sound occurs anywhere in the poem. The predominating vowels throughout are the broad or rounded ones: laurel, all, woods, no more. And so by contrast the tone rises almost beyond control in the "ai, ai"—"high wild woods".

The long-i sound itself is physiologically produced with greater muscular tension than the rounded vowels, and, although it can be uttered with a somewhat relaxed tongue, it can be, and very often is, tightened up by a very tense tongue position. It may often be observed when children are crying that their oo—and ah—vowel sounds represent a comparatively relaxed indulgence in tears, while the intense, partly withheld grief is more likely to be uttered in ai—or ee—sounds. The choruses of wailing women in Greek tragedy, too, often utter their grief in the crying of "ai". Thus, when other intensifying elements are present, this sound inevitably increases the tension. And so in the poem, by saying a simple thing with tension—tension brought about by technical or formal means—the unsaid is said.

Two other formal elements make this line stand out in the poem as a climax. For here more distinctly than anywhere else are heard three accents in juxtaposition, the "high wild woods". Elsewhere are slighter instances of the banking of accents: "the year draws in the day" and "woods no more". But they are less evenly and emphatically banked. And finally, this line, of all in the poem, is left unrhymed, a notable irregularity in the midst of convention.

The tension is drawn gradually, however, so that the reader feels the effect of it without being distinctly

aware of the means by which it is achieved. The slightly
more intense form of the first line when it recurs like a
musical enlargement,

> "Oh, we'll no more, no more
> To the leafy woods away,"

is the means: an interjection, a doubling of *no more*,
and a sharper picture and vowel sound in *leafy*—more
precise color and detail, that is, in contrast with the
somber prevailing tone, and a tense *ee*-sound which has
occurred only once before.

But the thing may be seen in reverse, too, for the poet
has used his meanings as elements of *form*. He has written a song of one theme in two parts: (A) *We shall not
go to the woods,* (B) *because it is too late (the laurels
are cut).* The two parts are distinct but bound together
by the common *woods-laurels.* The form will have to be
shown.

We'll to the woods no more,	A
The laurels all are cut,	B
The bowers are bare of bay That once the Muses wore;	B_1
The year draws in the day And soon will evening shut:	B_2
The laurels all are cut,	B
We'll to the woods no more.	A
Oh we'll no more, no more To the leafy woods away,	A_1
To the high wild woods of laurel And the bowers of bay no more.	A_2B_1

The formal balance of this is obvious. Its tonal unity is
made more complete by the prevailing *l*, *r*, and *w*

sounds, into which are fitted the contrasts of sound already mentioned.

Analysis like this may seem perhaps mechanical, and it does not, of course, reproduce the poet's way of constructing the poem. His ways are devious even to himself, and A. E. Housman has specifically said that very little in his poetry was produced by conscious effort. Analysis can only describe in a few obvious aspects the material pattern as finally produced in the poem. And it is certainly true, as Professor Alexander has said, that the poet does not know distinctly what the end-product is to be until it actually *is*. He does not map a pattern and then proceed to fill it out with words. But neither is this pattern a chance or arbitrary one. For its organization is in every detail related to its meaning, as we have partly seen here. Its greatness and perfection do not lie in the fact that the poet could construct this formal pattern representing unity in variety. It lies in the fact that the pattern seems to spring inevitably from the deepest meaning or feeling in the poem, and that it serves, while being a complete sound pattern in itself, to unite the content with its symbol. For if the symbol were all, if the poem meant no more than that the season for gathering green is over, the poet would not be driven to the extremes of contrast in form and sound, to the reiteration, the intensification, and the enlargement of the form. Just as in life we often know by a man's way of cherishing an object that it is not merely an object but is a symbol of something important to him, so here by Housman's way of cherishing the unimportant idea, he conveys to us without saying it—and indeed causes us to feel—the important meaning beneath.

In its final effect even the beautiful sound pattern of

itself *becomes* an added element of meaning. We are made to feel that since this pattern so perfectly conveys a meaning, it must in some hidden sense *be* that meaning—be it, that is, in a more real sense than merely even by being its inevitable analogue. If we literally believed that this was so, we should be growing pretty mystical. But what Coleridge called poetic faith, a "willing suspension of disbelief", is really our experience—one that we all recognize even if we cannot analyze it.

Our statement, therefore, that the primary meaning of Housman's poem is found in the poet's feeling about the end of his living work is true only in one sense. What made Housman write a poem instead of shedding tears or killing himself or dreaming bad dreams or telling his troubles to a friend—was the fact that for a time something else replaced pain as the center of his experience. Through some yet unexplained change, a change involving the whole meaning of *poet*, other things took on new light to his imagination, and a feeling of synthesis replaced in some degree that pain; everything seemed to be one: end of work, end of life, death of the year, all conceivable endings in fact, or even *ending* as an abstract idea. All that is different and yet not different, like a fugue in words, is united into identity. The experience then becomes a satisfying one, yet without destroying altogether the quality of pain in it.

This is essentially the same experience as the Aristotelian catharsis in tragedy, through pity and terror. Is it not possible that from among the painful human emotions these two occurred to Aristotle, not because they in fact are the primary feelings aroused by every tragedy, but rather because they are the two emotions utterly irreconcilable in real life? We cannot actually, I think, in our own life experience pity and terror at the same time: one drives the other out. But we can and do experience these or their analogues together—along with other emotions—in witnessing a tragedy. Precisely because of their irreconcilability in life we receive the greatest pleasure from their union in art. And so the pleasurable aesthetic feeling that results from the synthesis predominates easily over the painful character of the content without obliterating altogether the pain. It is through form, as we have tried to show very roughly in the case of Housman's poem, that this shift of value takes place: the painful becomes partially transformed through imaginative gratification of man's deep desire, the desire for unity of all things.

CHAPTER EIGHT

SUBJECT AND MOTIVE

Two of the oldest problems in the theory of art remain to us: the questions concerning standards of taste and limitation of subject matter. As to the latter, there is now little controversy. Except by a few critics, it is generally agreed that an artist has entire freedom of choice in his subject, that no subject is in itself unfit for art. But there is an important proviso attached to this freedom which is also generally, if tacitly, agreed upon, a proviso first clearly stated by Wordsworth in reference to a particular class of subjects. "The remotest discoveries of the Chemist, the Botanist, or Mineralogist, will be as proper objects of the Poet's art as any upon which it can be employed, *if the time should ever come when these things shall be familiar to us, and the relations under which they are contemplated by the followers of these respective sciences shall be manifestly and palpably material to us as enjoying and suffering beings.* If the time should ever come when what is now called science, thus familiarized to men, shall be ready to put on, as it were, a form of flesh and blood, the Poet will lend his divine spirit to aid the transfiguration, and will welcome the Being thus produced, as a dear and genuine inmate of the household of man." [1] Any subject, then, that matters to us as enjoying and suffering beings is a proper subject for art. And there is no conceivable portion of human experience that may not so matter to us.

All the other obvious things that have been said about subject matter remain true: that art is a mirror of civilization, its content changing with the social changes of each age; that the relatively permanent aspects of human nature are reflected in the more permanently valuable art, the fundamental things of life—love, death, the struggle to survive—constituting over and over its subject, in the most sophisticated as in the most primitive cultures.

But this is not all. Though in the bare choice of general subject the artist does have complete freedom, in the choice of all the details of content within any given work of art he is not quite so free. Here again there are no objectively defined classes of material that he may not include; but there is a principle of selection that he may not violate. If the effect he achieves is to be an aesthetic and not some other kind of effect, he must so select—as well as so present—his material that no other single meaning will overshadow or destroy the ultimate unification-meaning. This implies that some kinds of subjects are, though not impossible, dangerous for an aesthetic result. The artist runs a risk of having his own interest in one subject lead him out into the marketplace where his unifying control may cease. If this happens, he may produce something that has great social usefulness but that will not be art. In literature, few things have stirred as much controversy as this very situation in which a writer of ability uses a literary form or

[1] Preface to the second edition of the *Lyrical Ballads* [italics mine].

methods traditionally associated with aesthetic purposes, but uses them, either wittingly or unwittingly, to further action in a given cause or to create belief in a given set of ideas.

There is certainly no moral law against his doing this. If there is any objection to it, the objection can only be a practical one. But two results almost always follow. Readers to whom aesthetic experience is relatively unimportant, if they are sympathetic with the writer's views, will be impressed or pleased, perhaps even benefited morally or intellectually by what they have read. On the other hand, readers who value aesthetic experience highly and who have come to associate it inveterately with certain kinds of form—with the rhythmical form of poetry, for example—will very likely reject the work, perhaps with an imputation of perfidiousness to the author. Forms which have been long associated with the aesthetic and which have been found peculiarly suited to producing aesthetic impressions arouse such a strong expectation of that particular experience that the reader is not willing or able to take in any other if this one is lacking. His response is like that of the child who unexpectedly finds his orange juice mixed with quinine— no doubt for his own good if he will swallow it, but he probably will not. The result is generally the same whether the author has purposely used an art form to convey a non-aesthetic meaning, or whether he has been unintentionally led, by his own relation to the subject, into doing so.

This mere habitual association of form with aesthetic effect is not the only reason, however, that we tend to reject its use with a non-aesthetic purpose. The traditional forms of art, having been developed as unity-in-variety symbols, have an actual *meaning* in themselves, a content which is no more and no less than unification itself. If the artist's purpose is not primarily aesthetic, then this is not his meaning; and by using the forms of art he is saying what he does not intend. No wonder, then, that his work seems to the beholder to be "false" art, and that it arouses the same feelings of irritation and contempt that any kind of dishonesty arouses.

Very often, however, the result will be mixed: the effect of the whole will be one thing, that of some individual parts will be another. In the music of Wagner, for example, there are passages in which the erotic so overpowers other elements that the effect upon most hearers probably is not aesthetic. The musical construction of most of the scene, or of the opera, may be predominantly aesthetic; but the whole will be what we think of as imperfect art in consequence of these departures. Or, as in the thunderstorm of Beethoven's Pastoral Symphony, the composer as craftsman may seem to have been lured from his aesthetic purpose by the pure fun of solving a technical problem in imitation. And so the cuckoo sings before the storm, and the thunder and lightning resound; but except in some passages in which the composer's more usual artistic impulse is at work, we do not value that part of the composition for anything beyond its interest to an idle curiosity.

This is not to say, however, that a great deal of thought content, a great deal even of content that is meant to impel the reader toward action—toward furthering a personal, social, political, religious cause—may not be unified into an aesthetic whole by a person who is artist enough and whose own impulse toward the aesthetic is powerful enough to shape such content into art. But his aesthetic impulse has to be very powerful indeed for this, or his material will crash through and destroy his creation. To know that it can be done, we need only recall the poetry of Milton or Gerard Hopkins, or the great religious paintings of the past. With any of these artists, I think it may be taken as axiomatic that wherever he succeeded in producing art, he did so because his aesthetic motive dominated all other motives during the process of composition, whether he knew it or not. The odds seem to be against aesthetic success when the subject, taken purely as content, is immediately imperious or highly controversial. But the problem lies in the artist's attitude toward the subject and not in the subject itself. If his feeling is: *This is a subject that I ought to treat*, he will probably not produce art. But if it seems to him: *This is a subject that I could make something out of*, then he may. If his imagination, that is, becomes fired with the possibilities in terms of his own temperament, of a subject, as well as his conscience with its importance, then he may be able to produce an aesthetic result.

Present-day writers of the social revolution furnish us with endless matter for speculation on this point. They have an inheritance in one important respect different from that of any artists of the past. Though they perhaps scorn to acknowledge the influence, they are nevertheless living after and not before the "art for art's sake" movement of the eighties and nineties. This creed, discredited though it now is, has had a really profound effect upon our conception of the purposes of art, and for a very good reason. Not that we can now accept the creed; the phrase *art for art's sake*, has, I think, no meaning at all if inspected closely, any more than has the recent phrase of Clive Bell, who describes the purpose of art as the creation of "significant form" but refuses to say that the form is significant of anything. Both Bell and the art for art's sake aesthetes attracted a following because they clearly recognized aesthetic experience to be different in kind from other experience and because they recognized that the aesthetic value of an art product does not depend on the ostensible subject or ostensible meaning of the work. They quite obviously themselves enjoyed aesthetic experience, and they recognized it when they had it. But in taste they were narrow, and in theory they failed to look far enough. Rightly denying that the value of the *Faerie Queene* or of Michelangelo's figures in the Medici chapel lies in any obvious allegorical significance, the "aesthetes" went on to deny the aesthetic value of all meaning. Here they, and many of us since, erred.[1] We have been misled by the abstractness or vastness or generalized character of the meaning-value of works of art. The fundamental meaning of any aesthetic object lies so deep within us, is so generally implicit and not explicit in life, that it has been easily hidden behind the term *form* or behind the notion of contemplating an object for its own sake. Realizing that art is directed to no *practical* or *intermediate* end, and not realizing that its true end actually exists though buried almost out of sight among our instincts, we have fallen into the logical error of supposing it to be its own end.

It is not only the "aesthetes", however, who have placed modern propagandist artists in a different position from those of former times; it is perhaps not even this group chiefly. A great deal of thought on the part of philosophers, artists, and poets ever since the late eighteenth century has been at work to undermine the

[1] For example, A. E. Housman in *The Name and Nature of Poetry*.

almost universal ancient belief that art should instruct as well as please. But, especially in recent years, and especially in France, England, and America, under the cumulative force of the impressionists in painting, the French symbolists in literature, the *fin de siècle* aesthetics of Pater and Wilde in England, and even, in a small way, the now utterly forgotten Imagists in America—under the pressure of all this the "proletarian poets", who are nearly all persons of literary traditions, feel themselves on the defensive—as Tennyson never was when he wrote *The Princess*, or as Pope never was in conceiving the *Essay on Man*. Or as Milton never was.

Thus modern propagandist poets are far more distinctly conscious of their aesthetic problem and its pitfalls. But one hardly knows whether this has helped or hindered them. They have learned—partly from the psychologists and "educators"—that the best way to influence men is through use of concrete material, through illustration and example rather than abstract reasoning. They have been taught not to preach directly. Following these principles, and finding them reinforced by the predominantly concrete character of most great art, they have in many cases achieved something that looks a good deal like genuine poetry—though only on the surface. Too often when their "moral" is ushered into its concrete setting it gives an impression of discontinuity. The writer is apologetic about inserting his moral, or else he carries off his timidity about it by being bumptious and assertive. In either case the aesthetic effect fails: the moral and its concrete setting do not amalgamate. Or if he decides to rely upon the concrete altogether, leaving his moral implicit, then he nearly always produces a mass of heterogeneous material which might have been fused into artistic unity by imaginative indignation—supposing him to be presenting, say, the evils of capitalism—but which are not fused, because the poet's mind was occupied with the effect on his readers, and not with the effect on his "other self", which we have seen to be a condition of aesthetic production.

This indeed, as I see it, is the ultimate crux of all the problems of art-with-a-purpose. The aesthetic feeling of the creator is lost as soon as he ceases to write for his "objectified" self. He need not perhaps be thinking of this self alone: he may be thinking at the same time of fame or of improving or convincing the world. But whatever else may be in his mind in the way of audience, once he loses the sense that he is addressing that objectified self primarily, he loses his art. The moment Wordsworth inserts the vocative, "Reader"—in that moment and by that specific symptom do we know that his inspiration has left him. This is the real difference, subjectively described, between the aesthetic and the non-aesthetic motive in art so far as it relates to the utilitarian or propagandist controversy.

The effect upon the reader of propagandist literature, whether novel or poetry, in which the writer is no longer addressing himself but only the world, very often is that of an indirect insult or piece of condescension. The reader would say to the writer: "If you are willing to address this to me only in the shape in which you would have it preserved for your own self, then I know that you respect me as you do yourself. But if to impress me you must alter your original vision of your subject (supposing you ever to have had one); if to impress me you exaggerate, not because the situation creates an exaggerated image in your own mind, but making the horrible more horrible because you suppose it will take more to move me than it took to move you, or prettifying your message because you suppose that I have not the strength to bear what you have borne—if you do these things, then I know that you are condescending to me, and I am insulted. Moreover you are not then giving your best. Only if you imagine me, your reader, to be identical with your own best conceivable self—only then will your highest powers be called forth; only then will you create a great work of art. And only then shall I willingly hear what you have to say." Thus the aesthetic audience to the artist.

Wordsworth is a poet who has on different occasions both succeeded and failed in writing poetry-with-a-purpose. If it were not for offending the taste of those who still consider "We Are Seven" a fine example of his noble simplicity, I think it would be possible to show pretty accurately how a condescension in Wordworth's attitude here—not so much toward the child as toward the reader—makes him create a false simplicity, destroys even his standard of workmanship so that he is quite willing to force a rhyme or pad a line, to say the easiest thing that can be said within the given form—all because that other self, his proper and most exacting audience, has been entirely supplanted by merely the public who need to be taught a lesson.

But the same thing may be seen by comparing, for example, Wordsworth's "Lines on the Expected Invasion, 1803," with one of his better poems on a related subject. The familiar "London, 1802" sonnet will serve as well as any.

Milton! thou shouldst be living at this hour:
England hath need of thee: she is a fen
Of stagnant waters: altar, sword, and pen,
Fireside, the heroic wealth of hall and bower,
Have forfeited their ancient English dower
Of inward happiness. We are selfish men;
Oh! raise us up, return to us again;
And give us manners, virtue, freedom, power.
Thy soul was like a Star, and dwelt apart;
Thou hadst a voice whose sound was like the sea:
Pure as the naked heavens, majestic, free,
So didst thou travel on life's common way,
In cheerful godliness; and yet thy heart
The lowliest duties on herself did lay.

This is perhaps not among the greatest of all sonnets:
it has its prosaic moments. But it is good poetry; its
power is heard in the ring and echo of the fine cadences.
Here are the "Lines on the Expected Invasion, 1803".

Come ye—who, if (which Heaven avert!) the Land
Were with herself at strife, would take your stand,
Like gallant Falkland, by the Monarch's side,
And, like Montrose, make Loyalty your pride—
Come ye—who, not less zealous, might display
Banners at enmity with regal sway,
And, like the Pyms and Miltons of that day,
Think that a State would live in sounder health
If Kingship bowed its head to Commonwealth—
Ye too—whom no discreditable fear
Would keep, perhaps with many a fruitless tear,
Uncertain what to choose and how to steer—
And ye—who might mistake for sober sense
And wise reserve the plea of indolence—
Come ye—whate'er your creed—O waken all,
Whate'er your temper, at your Country's call;
Resolving (this a free-born Nation can)
To have one Soul, and perish to a man,

Or save this honoured Land from every Lord
But British reason and the British sword.

This is prosaic throughout. Except for the almost
appalling jerkiness of movement, its poetic weakness is
not as easily demonstrated as in "We Are Seven", because the weakness does not lie primarily in its workmanship. But the whole is too expository to be poetic.
Wordsworth is too intent upon explaining to us, his
readers, what different classes of people he means to
summon by his call to arms. He tries to do this poetically
by being circuitous, by saying, for "seventeenth century
Royalists",

"...ye—who, if (which Heaven avert!) the Land
Were with herself at strife, would take your stand,
Like gallant Falkland, by the Monarch's side,
And, like Montrose, make Loyalty your pride—"

Because he is not showing something new to himself
but only (he hopes) to the less enlightened public, his
poetic diction is circuitous without being suggestive; it
has no more richness or variousness of implied meaning
than the direct prose statement would have. If that ideal
other self had been his prime audience, it would have
required of him something less external and less insignifi-
cant than the material by which he built up the meaning
of this poem. The literal meaning is neither trivial nor
insincere (though one may think it mistaken); but the
poem itself is clearly addressed outward instead of inward. Because the feeling behind it is not primarily
aesthetic there is neither poetic suggestiveness in the
words nor harmony in the cadences of the verse, though
it is written by a poet capable of creating both.

To those young artists of social conscience who ardently

desire to further the causes of the new world by their art, who wonder whether it is possible or who determine that it shall be possible to create a great art out of revolutionary material—to these artists there is no ready-made theoretical answer. Surely it will be possible *if or when* there arises a fully endowed artist who, however powerful his social motive and sympathy, is yet in creative work governed primarily by an aesthetic motive. Whether such an artist's work would be aided by his having a clearer intellectual understanding of the nature of aesthetic experience than was available in former times, is a question that I think none of us can answer with certainty. Such an understanding might, I think, prevent a talented artist from producing artistically poor work. But that is no guarantee that it would enable him to produce the opposite.

There is a second class of subjects that are full of pitfalls if one aims to produce a work of art, the kind of subject in which the artist is intimately and personally involved and concerning which his own feelings are in conflict. Artistic failure from this source has been more frequent in literature since the beginning of the romantic movement than before it, because since then we have come to accept more personal subjects as fit for art. And there is nothing wrong, of course, with the subjects in themselves. But they often tempt the poet or novelist (for it is with these two artists that the problem most often occurs) to make use of his reader as a confidant or an aid of some kind to the solving of his own problems. He "takes out on the reader" whatever may be wrong with himself. If he writes for his "other self", it is not his ideal but a worse or weaker self. There have been two conspicuous instances of this in recent literature, the novels of D. H. Lawrence and the less well-known sonnet sequence, *Two Lives*, of William Ellery Leonard. The work of these men attracted attention, both sympathetic and hostile, partly in consequence of the freedom with which they communicated their personal problems to the reader. They have been greeted as great artists by many critics, and there is indeed no denying that Lawrence, at least, had all the gifts of a great writer. But he had neither the conscience nor the intention of an artist and should not therefore have used art forms. Had he written, instead, unvarnished autobiography, or had he kept a diary like Pepys, we should have had from him a work of permanent worth. As it is, he climbs in and out of the novel form, using it without conviction. He goes out of his way at one moment, for instance, to make his heroine specifically and pointedly Irish, so that the reader must visualize her and take in as significant her very Irishness. But later on the author has forgotten that he made her Irish; she is an Englishwoman. This is what we mean by the lack of artistic conscience in Lawrence. It is not that we mind mere inconsistency as such. If a character in a novel leaves for Europe and is back before a ship could have brought him, we are not greatly disturbed: we merely recall Shakespeare's Bohemian seacoast. But here, without justification, he demands of the reader such attention and belief as are only justified by a genuine artistic motive. The confusion shows in his very style. Nearly all the writing in his novels, in fact, falls between two not clearly defined intentions, an expository and a dramatic intention; so that the reader is constantly being called upon for belief in dramatic illusion, when all that the author at bottom desires to say is expository.

The case of Leonard's *Two Lives* is simpler. Apart from its diffuseness and its prevailingly undistinguished style and thought, it fails fundamentally by reason of a non-aesthetic purpose. However much the original intention may have been aesthetic, it is only too clear that during the actual writing, Leonard's mind was ridden by the need to justify himself. He seizes the reader by the ear to convince him. "My neighbors blame me; but you, my reader, must be made to understand that I am not at fault. If I can convince you, perhaps I may believe it myself." And so the reader is made use of to solve the writer's own inner problem. The result is a painful piece of self revelation, more being revealed than the author intends or desires. The effect has nothing to do with aesthetic experience except negatively—except, that is, as the use of poetic form offends the reader's sense of fitness and his aesthetic expectations.

These instances are typical of what happens, not precisely when an artist chooses a subject unfit for artistic treatment, but when he chooses a subject the dangers of which are too great for his power—his power over the emotional problems involved, not necessarily the technical ones. And it is still true that, given a great enough man, animated by a strong enough aesthetic motive, anything can be turned into art, even the innermost confusion of his own soul. Witness Shakespeare's sonnets or the tragic sonnets of Gerard Hopkins.

CHAPTER NINE

"TASTE" [1]

This, then, brings us to a final question. If the motive of aesthetic experience is as we have described it, and if any man may find aesthetic experience almost anywhere in life, can there possibly be any meaning in the search for standards of taste in the arts? Should we ever speak of good and bad taste? Or can any criteria ever be established that will compel agreement? Repeat as often as we like *de gustibus non est disputandum*, we yet always do dispute concerning tastes and we have an apparently unquenchable desire that others should accept our own standards. It is not enough that x gives one of us individually more aesthetic satisfaction than y or that x gives us some pleasure and y none. We insist that the experience of others ought to be the same as our own.

If we analyze this desire of ours, however, I think we shall find that it tends to break into two strands; that is, in part we *require* agreement, and in part we should like but do not require it. In music, one may prefer Bach to Mozart, but one does not insist that others should. In such a case as this, a man is pleased if others share his preference, but only because he likes the sympathetic

<hr />

[1] For much of the framework of this discussion I am indebted to the first and the final chapters of Barrows Dunham's *A Study of Kant's Aesthetics*, Lancaster, 1933.

sharing of any experience. On the other hand, let us say he also prefers Bach to MacDowell, and here he does require that all others agree with him; if they do not, he considers them "wrong". Or, again, one may prefer Chaucer to Keats, or the reverse, without requiring agreement of others. But in preferring Shakespeare's sonnet sequence to William Ellery Leonard's, or—to be a trifle less outrageous—in preferring A. E. Housman's poems to Leonard's, we again require agreement of others.

The degree to which universal agreement in matters of art can be or is demanded, depends, I believe, upon two things, both of which may be definitely formulated —though formulation is the beginning rather than the end of problems of disagreement. In the first place, *as far as agreement is required in other areas of value— moral, social, intellectual, even sensuous—so far the same agreement is demanded in the values of art.*

Thus, if our general philosophy is an absolute one—if we believe that there is an absolute scale of values for the whole of life either already determined or else determinable, we must identify the value of works of art according to these. And whether we are absolutist or relativist, just as far as we are willing to say that all men ought to be alike, so far do we demand that all men's taste in art should be alike. Insofar as we agree that men should be as ethical in intention as possible, as intelligent, as strong, as sensitive, as capable of depths of experience—so far do we also agree upon what ought to be regarded as the higher or the lower in art. And wherever we still vary in these criteria, there do our artistic standards vary also.

What we have just said is true, however, only when modified by two important conditions. For, in the first place, these judgments of value are relevant only after it has been decided whether the effect of a given work is aesthetic or non-aesthetic in character. This judgment has to be made separately for each work because the aesthetic, even in art, is so mingled with other things that it is not always and instantly recognized by everyone. Many men have not learned to isolate their own aesthetic experience clearly enough to be able to recognize consciously and precisely the kind of experience it is. This is often the case even with intelligent and well-informed people, people whom the world might look upon as judges in such matters, but in whose lives real aesthetic experience has not played a very important part. Such persons—and they are many—are likely to suppose that any satisfaction they receive from any of the arts is aesthetic in character. They express this satisfaction in terms of aesthetic judgment; that judgment is respected; and we therefore have even more confusion than we need have in the standards by which art is judged.

For certainly some of this confusion is needless. As was remarked earlier, aesthetic experience is not an essential of life—that is, it is not necessary for survival and it is, no doubt, even taking into consideration all that is known of primitive art, a comparatively late human development. It has therefore remained unanalyzed and unidentified by intellectual apprehension somewhat longer than other important areas of experience. But it can be recognizably described, and has been; and I think general agreement on its special identity may gradually be established. When this occurs, some at least of our present confusion in criticism will be obviated. We might pretty generally agree, for instance, that a book by D. H. Lawrence is not art, but that it is both valuable and interesting because it provides new and striking sources for the understanding of human beings. Such clarification and definition might even help artists themselves to realize just when they really desire to create a work of art, and when they desire to do something else.

We require agreement, then, upon the primary classification of a work: is it art, or is it not art? By this we must mean: Is it peculiarly fitted to give aesthetic pleasure? And further: Is it fitted to give aesthetic pleasure that has more or less the same content for everyone who enjoys it? The criterion can never be that a work shall invariably give pleasure. In this it differs from any criterion in the moral world. For one may insist, in the moral world, that everyone should be interested in furthering the good; but one neither does nor ought to insist that everyone must be interested in music. This distinction exists, of course, because the primary value of the aesthetic is to the individual whereas the primary value of the moral is to society. And so in the judgment of art we can say only that it is calculated to and tends to, and, under favorable circumstances, will produce aesthetic pleasure. The definition is in functional and not categorical terms, like the definition of a seed as something which *if* planted, *if* watered, *if*—innumerable other conditions are fulfilled—will reproduce that from which it came. The definition is functional and conditional, but not altogether indefinite.

Within the realm of what has been judged to be aesthetic in character, then, we have said that we demand further identity of judgment, in the same degree as we demand it in other areas of value. But the relation between aesthetic and, again, moral values is not the simple ratio of *the more morality (in the painter or in his picture) the better art.* To suppose this is to forget the whole motive of art, its imaginative unification. It is true that the one set of values depends upon the others, but rather in this way: *the greater the conflict and variety, and the greater the importance of the elements unified by a given work, or the greater the problem for us in the conflict of these elements ununified, the greater is the art which unifies them.* And, on the other hand, also: *the more striking and consistent, and the more complete the unity of diverse content, the greater is the art.*[1] Or it might be reduced to this: the more improbable the unity achieved, the greater the art. Which is what Keats no doubt felt when he said that poetry should surprise by a fine excess, and what Gerard Hopkins more clearly referred to in his statement that "in everything the more remote the ratio of the parts to one another or the whole the greater the unity if felt at all." Those problems that press hardest for solution, those meanings and conflicts that tease by their intangibility, those diversities that we should like but have never hoped to bring together—the relative value of those, and the intensity and completeness of their union gives us our scale of value in art, definite and indefinite as those other values are.

But this scale of values, double as it already is, becomes further complicated by another fact about artistic production, the fact that aesthetic unification is often achieved in parts or brief passages while it is lost in other passages or in the construction of the whole. And the value that men place upon art of this kind varies greatly

---

[1] These two criteria, incidentally, may perhaps be seen to mark the most fundamental distinction between what we call the romantic and the classic in art.

with their individual temperament. To some readers the beautiful wholeness and perfection of a single line of poetry or a single image will outweigh any number of imperfections in the rest of the poem. To others it will not. This difference in the judgment of art traces back to differences in our sets of values in life itself. None but the most extreme absolutist philosopher, I think, will hope that there can ever be identity of judgment in this respect. Even at best, then, we are still doomed to a wilderness of personal preferences.

As a corollary, however, of the principles we have laid, one other requirement follows, which I think ought to be recognized in theory as it always has been in the practice of artists. It is this. We demand that neither the content of a work of art nor the form shall be too simple or too single. This idea may at first glance appear strange, inasmuch as we often praise art for the very quality of simplicity. Yet it may be shown, I think, that this is a necessary law and a law that the great artist obeys so automatically that no critic ever has to tell him about it. It is also a law that the inferior artist is constantly breaking.

To return once more to the boy with his peg and hole. The question might have been raised: Why—seeing that the various symbolic meanings of his action were of deep and universal significance—why was not his action a work of great art? or at least why was the aesthetic experience that it gave him a mere slight and passing one, scarcely indeed noticeable? The primary reason I think must be that his action was both too easy and too simple to constitute a satisfactory symbol for all the meanings that it faintly suggested. The complexities of life, we feel, are great and not easily solved or unified; and we demand of any symbol intended to represent their unification that it represent also something of the complexity. We demand more even than this. For as the union of the many into the one seems to us a kind of miracle, we require that, to give us great pleasure, a symbol representing it shall present an aspect so difficult or so complex or so improbable that it will seem itself like a miracle. Otherwise the symbol will strike us as false or misleading, as not truly representing that which it purports to represent. This demand of ours is the basis for much of our objection to art that we call sentimental. Its synthesis is too easy to be true, and so the symbol is false. Or, from the technical angle, when we object to the versification of some inferior poem on the ground of monotony, what we really object to is less the monotony than the simplicity of the form. We say it is "obvious", that its devices and effects are too easy to account for. Or we merely call it "cheap".

On two grounds, in fact, really simple simplicity is unacceptable in art: in the first place, because it generally renders the symbol false, and in the second, because—if it does not do this—it makes the work too easily apprehended by the *intellect*. Coleridge was not altogether fantastic in saying that "poetry gives most pleasure when only generally and not perfectly understood". Art, as has been said before, deals with that which is felt to be unknown. The moment that form, content, implications, and the relation between all these are actually known or felt to be known, at that moment the aesthetic effect ceases. We err, therefore, when we suppose, as we commonly do, that the "intellectual" enjoyer of art, who prefers the most intellectually complex music of Bach to the simplest of folk music, prefers this "because he can understand it". The truth is rather that when the music is complex it is easier for him not to be too conscious of how it is put together. I think, in fact, it will be found that the only simple art is inferior art and that all great art, even that which we customarily regard as simple, is actually complex, either through a multiplicity of expressed and suggested meanings or of associations and relations between meanings, or else by virtue of structural complexity which in itself represents other complexities.

Nothing could be more simple in appearance than the poem of Housman that we have discussed, "We'll to the Woods No More". Yet we have seen something, and might see much more, of its structural complexity. The same thing is true, I think, of the "simplicities" of the best of Blake or Herrick.

Perhaps the truly simple may appear in art successfully if it forms part of a larger unit, in which its effect is that of contrast with surrounding elements so that the whole is therefore still complex in effect. This is sometimes the case in the sonatas of Beethoven. Here the prevailing mood almost always has something weightily responsible about it; and against this the occasional streaks of simplicity (not always as simple in pattern as they look, it is true) shine out, making the whole all the more complex. That is what the hymn of joy in the Ninth Symphony was obviously intended to do. As a matter of fact—though this is a heretical opinion—I think that the joy theme fails of its intended effect, and fails by reason of its too simple and obvious structure. It should have been the arrow of lightning that stamps a seal of finality upon the whole gigantic and complex frame. But it is too predictable: once begun, the structure of the theme is obvious and the hearer can very nearly invent the remainder for himself. The result is a certain flatness of effect that does not reinforce but rather damages the impressiveness of the whole.

Thus we demand, for any important aesthetic experience, complexity and even, in a certain sense, difficulty. It need not be the difficulty of the moderns—of Hopkins, Eliot, Joyce—who have rendered almost inaccessible what used to be always overt in meaning. But if it is art it must require skill. If it is the deceptively simple poetry of Burns, we must find ourselves amazed that from the welter of the commonplace—this particular, most special, utterly expressive combination of meanings and sounds has been chosen. In the enjoyment of natural beauty it is the same. If we experience any intensity of pleasure, we must do so because the scene or object strikes us as something unusual or as something most highly specialized, like the form of a flower; and it must suggest to us the terrific odds against so special an object's having occurred by mere chance. It is always something that seems to us—though we know better—most difficult for nature to have achieved. For there is always a sense of wonder attached to aesthetic experience.

We can thus explain one of the common anomalies of aesthetic appreciation. We all know and feel rather superior to the kind of person who receives genuine aesthetic pleasure from a conventional postcard photograph of, say, a moonlit lake. Upon those who are accustomed to receive aesthetic pleasure from the arts or from nature, such a picture has no effect. They know quite well that no special skill or insight was required to take it. Their sense of wonder is not aroused; nothing induces them to look through the picture to the original scene, which might have aroused it. But the person who is unaccustomed to receiving aesthetic pleasure from art or nature, who probably "does not know anything about art" and who when he is in the country has never acquired the habit of being in what we call a pre-aesthetic mood—such a person is nevertheless quite suggestible. The mere fact that someone has photographed the scene makes him know that this has been thought to be beautiful. So he falls into a pre-aesthetic mood, and in looking at the picture sees with his ready sense of wonder the scene beyond—which if he had seen it in real life might have meant nothing to him except as it reminded him of a previously seen (and hence chosen by someone else) photograph. Even here, then, where the aesthetic judgment of individuals differs most radically, one believing the picture to be beautiful and another not, the foundation of the experience is the same. It remains true even for the untrained and more simple-minded beholder that the aesthetic experience does not arise out of the perception of the simple, but must rest upon the complex, the improbable, the difficult-to-be-achieved. Only, our conception of the complex, the improbable, and the difficult, varies with our past experience in art and in life, and varies also with the direction, both at the moment and in the past, of our attention.

CHAPTER TEN

TRUTH AND ILLUSION

THE foregoing discussion does not, of course, constitute a complete theory of aesthetics. It is only a discussion of certain problems of art from a particular point of view; and it rests upon a central conception which is by no means novel, the unity-in-variety theory being as old as any in the world. But unity-in-variety has been nearly always the property of mystics. To others it has seemed an inadequate or an arbitrary theory because inexplicable in any but superficial terms. Why, they wonder, should the idea of the many-in-one be so important to us that it could motivate all artistic achievement? What could be its significance, unless one reads it as a definition of God or of the relation between God and his creation? And yet time after time artists themselves, whether mystics or not, come back to the idea, stating it in various ways but still seeing it as the central fact, each of his own art. Almost endless are the statements of it that might be compiled from their own lips.

The point of view upon which this discussion rests appears to me to give a little more solidity to such an interpretation of the aesthetic motive. The unifying impulse so obviously behind much of the work of man is an impulse not observable in, or deducible from the activity of other animals; and the same is true of aesthetic impulse and activity. Are they not fundamentally related? Moreover, the more closely one attempts to distinguish between that which is generally felt to be aesthetic and that which is not, the more, as I think we have seen here, this imaginative unity-in-variety appears to mark the primary difference. But—what is at least as important for aesthetic theory and perhaps also more demonstrable—when the subject is approached from this angle a good many of the old contradictions that have plagued aestheticians disappear or become explicable.

Some of these we have seen in passing. Others might here be elaborated, except that this would involve an almost intolerable repetition of theory already stated and restated. There is the "fitness" theory, for example—an idea commonly held in regard to architecture and the other useful arts, and often extended so as to define beauty in general: that beauty consists in the palpable fitness of a thing for its end. But such a theory cannot be made the basis of all art, for it cannot conceivably be made to account intelligibly for music. Yet it finds its place within our more general framework, when we see that the fitness of a thing for its end may become a perfect symbol to the mind of something else—of a unity of means and ends in general, for instance. Often pleasure in the fitness of a thing is felt in a degree far out of proportion to the actual end or value of the fitness. I am pleased, let us say, by an obviously perfect balance in weight between the handle and spout of a pitcher, far beyond the mere advantage of its reduced liability to upsetting. But unless this fitness is felt as a symbol of something else, I cannot explain why the mere fitness should give me a pleasure which I feel to be far more important than its usefulness alone would warrant.

The greatest objection that might be raised to this unification-of-reality theory I think might be to the prominent place that has been given the terms *symbol* and *illusion;* for it is easy then to conclude, if art is all symbol and illusion, that those who either create or enjoy art are merely "escaping from life". And no one to whom aesthetic experience is important wishes to have the psychological tag of "escape mechanism" affixed to his pleasure. Moreover he feels a positive value and importance in the experience that such a tag, with its at least superficially negative implication, wholly fails to account for.

To see how far true aesthetic experience differs from what is clearly an "escape"—escape in a genuinely negative sense—we have only to inspect a human activity that looks a little like art but is not. The daydream has been regarded by Freudians as the prototype of artistic creation, and the daydream is admittedly in part if not altogether a device for escaping the present and its responsibilities. Whether or not the daydream furnishes much of the subject matter of art—a point which there is very little evidence for determining at the present time —there are two important and characteristic differences between it and the aesthetic. The first, the comparative formlessness of daydreams, has been regularly taken into account by psychological writers. The artist is recognized as one who imposes form or unity upon the flowing process of the daydream.

The other difference, which has not been recognized, is one which sets art apart from any ordinary escape mechanism. It is this. Our daydreams we at least half believe in, *with a self-interested belief*; the creations of art, however compelling the illusion they produce, are never believed in in this manner—or if they are, the experience can be recognized as different from the aesthetic even by the person who has it. This is the distinction that was intended earlier when art was said to create *illusion* but not *delusion*; it is a difference hard to define accurately in words, but very clear and easy to feel. When the two kinds of belief become mingled in an art-form, as they often do, or when the first—the daydream belief—tends to supplant the other, then we do have what we all recognize as "escapist" art; but that means that, whatever the form, it is not really art at all, or at any rate it is not producing what we have called aesthetic experience.

Let us take, for example, what we might suppose to be the daydream of some dull and credulous young stenographer. She imagines that one day the handsome young son of a millionaire client enters the office—and so on. The situation that would be described at this point might equally well be taken from the girl's actual daydream or from any of the serial novels that she reads in the daily paper. The point is that both—daydream or story—she recognizes to be untrue *at the present time*, but both give her a feeling of specific hopefulness *that this very thing may actually happen to her in the future*. Her judgment of probabilities has become in some degree false; her actions in real life are altered by this false judgment. She begins to buy clothes, to practice speech and tones of voice suited to the story and not to herself.

This is an effect that aesthetic experience itself does not produce; and this is why we say that, though art creates illusion, neither the artist when he is creating nor the enjoyer of art is, by the fact of his activity, self-deceived about life. Art is indeed, in this sense, disinterested, as has so often been said. And the artistic temperament I think is no more subject to self-deception or escape than any other—even the scientific.

It is true that certain art-forms have been found particularly favorable modes of self-deception. But, when the form is used in this way, the production has always in the end been condemned as not art or as "bad art". Painting, poetry—any form, indeed, that is in some degree imitative—but most commonly of all, prose fiction, may be used or misused in this way. Whether it is through charm or through Victorian virtue that the young lady wins the rich husband, the effect is the same —an easy and false wish-fullfilment for the reader, who is led *to bring the story over prospectively into her own life* and so to deceive herself. The past is full of these corpses of literature. Mrs. Hannah More in the nineteenth century wrote endless books of goody-fiction, a mixture of escape and morality. In fact, wherever the desire to influence other people becomes a dominant motive of the artist—whether he desires to improve their morals, to awaken them to a public wrong, to encourage them in action, or to satisfy their appetites—there the likelihood that aesthetic illusion will pass over into delusion is probably strongest. But great art offers no false hopes to the individual.

Art, then, as far as it serves what we have called the aesthetic need of man—and this provision coincides very closely with what in the long run is universally recognized to be genuine art—is symbolic and illusory. It is illusory, in the sense in which I have used the term, even when it is "realistic", since the form is imposed upon life by the artist's vision and not by life itself. But it is not on this account either false or misleading or irresponsible.

On the other hand, we cannot say, as many to whom art is important would like to, that the artist is always the bearer of great truth to mankind, or that his function is to see farther into universal truth than the rest of us, and to convey to us this insight. Certainly he may do this. The greatest artists sometimes appear to be men in whom unusually strong intellectual power is united with unusual capacity for deep feeling and with unusual keenness of the senses. When this occurs, such an artist does indeed give us glimpses into truth—of life, of character, even of abstractions perhaps—that we have not had before. Every one, I suppose, has understood himself and others the better for having read *Hamlet*; has understood more clearly than before one way in which a man can go to pieces, from having read *Lear*; has understood (to take a modern instance) how that which had seemed intolerable can become tolerable, from reading Thomas Mann's account of Joseph in the pit; has understood the better how certain lines of face or posture betray a character, from seeing portraits by Modigliani. But, in the first place, this gain of insight is not the central experience which the art gives us: this is only a part of its content and not the prime thing that we value it for. And in the second place, not all great art gives it to us. If we individually value aesthetic experience highly, we are somewhat tempted, it is true, to build up the importance of the aesthetic by making this our general claim for it. But I do not think that we are entitled to do so. On the one hand, such a claim

would force us to rule out much that has stood the test
of time and criticism—the beautiful light lyrics of Robert
Herrick, for example. Or else, on the other hand, it
would compel us to stretch the meaning of the terms
truth and *insight* to a point which would render them
pretty useless for any other purpose. In the instances cited
above from Shakespeare, or Mann, we do indeed gain
insight into truth in an accepted sense of those terms.
Is it still insight into truth that we gain when Gerard
Hopkins makes us remember sleepless nights by writing,
"I wake and feel the fell of dark, not day"? Perhaps—
probably. But what becomes of the terms *truth* and *insight* if we make the same claim for Shakespeare in a
different mood?

> Full fathom five thy father lies;
> Of his bones are coral made;
> Those are pearls that were his eyes:
> Nothing of him that doth fade
> But doth suffer a sea-change
> Into something rich and strange.
> Sea nymphs hourly ring his knell:
> ding-dong.
> Hark! now I hear them,—ding-dong, bell.

Or if we assert that music, being an art, gives us insight
into truth? No; we shall have to give up the claim for
the artist that by virtue of being an artist he is a bringer
of new truth to man. He may be or he may not.

Having disposed of falsehood and of truth in relation
to art, we are more or less forced back upon that third
of the old familiar dogmas: that "art has nothing to do
with true or false, good or bad". This we may agree to.
But having arrived at it from a different direction we do

not have to choke ourselves with either of two contradictory corollaries, one or other of which is usually attached to this view: either that "art has nothing to do with life", a statement which seems quite meaningless; or that art deals only with the sensuous aspect of things—which I think is demonstrably false.

But enough of these arguments. Art will go on as long as man does. We need not be disturbed by the old worry, which the industrial revolution and Darwinism hatched in the minds of poet and critic, that knowledge or science would end by destroying the arts. Science and art each has its indestructible place in life. Neither satisfies us altogether, science because it never reaches its goal, and art because it can never retain its goal more than momentarily. Unless—or until—all things become known, and man thereby becomes God, or until evolution makes of man a different animal from that which he now is, he will make for himself art as well as science. And as long as we have art, we shall have theories of art, each generation its own, partly old and partly new, and never, we may suppose, final so long as any mystery remains in the mind of man or in the external world that surrounds him.